Dividend Stock Trading for Beginners

How to Grow Your Income and Generate Tremendous Profit
Trading Dividend Stocks

ABBEY LINCOLN

TABLE OF CONTENTS

Introduction

You must have dreamed of generating passive income that can grow into a sizeable stream of cash flow over time. Dividend stock investing offers beginners precisely that powerful opportunity. By learning how to identify, buy, and hold high-quality dividend-paying stocks, you can steadily build a portfolio that delivers rising dividend payments year after year. When combined with the magic of compounding through dividend reinvestment, even modest initial investment amounts can snowball into a prolific income-generating engine.

In this comprehensive introductory guide, you will discover the fundamentals of dividend stock trading and how to harness its wealth-building potential. You will learn to demystify dividends and compare dividend stocks versus growth stocks using key metrics. You will learn how to assess your financial goals, risk tolerance, and timeline to develop an investment plan tailored for you.

You will also uncover the power of setting up a dividend reinvestment plan (DRIP) to accelerate your compounding returns. You will find tips on managing taxes, legal considerations, and regulatory compliance as a dividend investor. Since psychology plays a huge role in trading success, you will also learn to overcome biases and cultivate the proper mindset. Finally, you will learn more advanced dividend trading strategies to further diversify your dividend streams.

While dividend trading comes with inherent risks that require prudence, this book will set you up for success by teaching you how to mitigate risks through diversification, analysis, loss-prevention strategies, and maintaining realistic expectations. You will learn key risk management techniques. Far from a get-rich-quick scheme, dividend trading rewards commitment, discipline, adaptability, and perspective. By mastering the evergreen principles in this book and sticking to proven best practices, you can consistently grow your portfolio and income year after year.

Imagine building enough dividend income to afford that dream vacation, purchase a comfortable retirement, or pursue your passion. Instead of struggling paycheck to paycheck, dividend trading can stabilize and grow your finances through steady, recurring cash flow. You can take control of your financial future and achieve true financial freedom. Whether you are a complete beginner or have some experience, this book aims to become your comprehensive guide to mastering dividend stock trading. By following the advice laid out in these chapters and applying it diligently, you will gain the skills and knowledge to generate tremendous profits through dividend stocks. There has never been a better time to begin your journey. Let's get started!

Chapter 1

Introduction to Dividend Stock Trading

Dividend stock trading is a strategy that involves investing in companies that pay dividends to their shareholders. Dividends are payments that companies make to distribute a portion of their earnings to their investors. Dividend stock trading can provide a steady source of income and capital appreciation for investors who are looking for long-term returns.

Significance of Dividend Stocks in Investment

Dividend stocks are important for investors who want to achieve both income and wealth goals. Here are some of the benefits of dividend stocks:

1. **Dividends Can Become a Regular Source of Income**: Dividend stocks can provide a consistent and predictable stream of cash flow for investors. Unlike interest payments from bonds or capital gains from selling stocks, dividends are not affected by market fluctuations or interest rate changes. Dividends can also increase over time if the company raises its dividend payout ratio or dividend growth rate. Investors can use dividends to supplement their income, reinvest in more shares, or diversify their portfolios.

2. **Dividends Contribute to Building Wealth:** Dividend stocks can also enhance the long-term returns of investors by compounding their growth. Compounding is the process of earning interest on interest, or in this case, earning dividends on dividends. By reinvesting dividends, investors can increase their number of shares and their future dividend income. Over time, this can result in a significant increase in the value of their investment. According to a study by Morningstar, dividends accounted for about 40% of the total return of the S&P 500 index from 1930 to 2012.

Dividend Stocks vs. Growth Stocks

Dividend stocks and growth stocks are two types of stocks that have different characteristics and objectives. Here are some of the differences between them:

1. Dividend stocks are stocks that pay dividends to their shareholders regularly. Dividend stocks tend to be from mature and stable companies that have established earnings and cash flows. Dividend stocks are suitable for investors who are looking for income, safety, and moderate growth.

2. Growth stocks are stocks that have a high potential for growth in their earnings and revenues. Growth stocks tend to be from young and innovative companies that reinvest their profits into expanding their business. Growth stocks are suitable for investors who are looking for capital appreciation, risk, and high returns.

Criteria	Dividend Stocks	Growth Stocks
Definitions	Stocks that pay dividends to their shareholders regularly	Stocks that have high potential for growth in their earnings and revenues
Examples	Coca-Cola, Johnson & Johnson, Procter & Gamble	Amazon, Tesla, Netflix
Benefits	Provide income, stability, and moderate growth	Provide capital appreciation, risk, and high returns
Risks	Dividend cuts, low growth, high valuation	Market volatility, earnings disappointment, high valuation
Dividend yield	High (usually above 3%)	Low (usually below 1%) or none
Dividend payout ratio	Moderate to high (usually between 40% to 80%)	Low (usually below 20%) or none
Dividend growth rate	Low to moderate (usually between 5% to 15%)	High (usually above 20%) or none
Earnings growth rate	Low to moderate (usually between 5% to 15%)	High (usually above 20%)
Price-to-earnings ratio	Low to moderate (usually between 10 to 25)	High (usually above 25)
Investment goals	Income, safety, and long-term returns	Capital appreciation, risk, and short-term returns

To decide which type of stock matches your investment goals, you need to consider your risk tolerance, time horizon, and income needs. Here are some questions to ask yourself:

- How much risk can you tolerate? Dividend stocks are generally less risky than growth stocks, as they provide a cushion of income and stability in volatile markets. Growth stocks are riskier as they depend on the future performance and expectations of the company. Growth stocks can also experience sharp price swings and corrections.

- How long do you plan to hold your investment? Dividend stocks are more suitable for long-term investors who want to benefit from the compounding effect of reinvesting dividends. Growth stocks are more suitable for short-term investors who want to capitalize on the rapid growth of the company.

- How much income do you need from your investment? Dividend stocks can provide a steady and reliable source of income for investors who need cash flow or passive income. Growth stocks do not pay dividends, as they reinvest their earnings into growing their business. Growth stocks can provide higher returns, but only if the investor sells them at a higher price than they bought them.

Benefits and Risks of Dividend Stock Trading

Investing in dividend stocks has many benefits for beginners who want to start their journey in the stock market. Some of the advantages of investing in dividend stocks are:

1. **Dividend Income:** Dividend stocks provide a regular and reliable source of income for investors. Unlike other sources of income, such as interest or capital gains, dividends are not affected by market fluctuations or interest rate changes. Dividends can also increase over time if the company raises its dividend payout ratio or dividend growth rate. Investors can use dividends to supplement their income, reinvest in more shares, or diversify their portfolios.

2. **Capital Appreciation**: Dividend stocks can also offer capital appreciation for investors who are looking for long-term growth. Dividend stocks tend to be from mature and stable companies that have established earnings and cash flows. These companies can withstand economic downturns and maintain their competitive advantage. Dividend stocks can also benefit from the compounding effect of reinvesting dividends, which can increase the number of shares and the future dividend income.

3. **Tax Advantages**: Dividend stocks can also provide tax advantages for investors who are eligible for lower tax rates on qualified dividends. Qualified dividends are dividends that meet certain criteria, such as being paid by a U.S. corporation or a foreign corporation that is eligible for tax treaty benefits. Qualified dividends are taxed at a lower rate than ordinary income, which can range from 0% to 20%, depending on the investor's tax bracket.

4. **Risk Reduction**: Dividend stocks can also reduce the risk of investing in the stock market by providing a cushion of income and stability. Dividend stocks tend to have lower volatility than growth stocks, as they are less sensitive to market swings and earnings surprises. Dividend stocks can also provide a hedge against inflation, as they can increase their dividends to match or exceed the rising prices. Dividend stocks can also protect investors from losing their principal, as they can recover their initial investment through dividends over time.

Here are some of the risks of investing in dividend stocks:

1. **Dividend Cuts**: Dividend stocks are not guaranteed to pay dividends forever. Companies can reduce or eliminate their dividends if they face financial difficulties, such as declining earnings, cash flow problems, or debt obligations. Dividend cuts can hurt the income and value of dividend stocks and the investor's confidence and trust in the company.

2. **Low Growth:** Dividend stocks tend to have lower growth potential than growth stocks, as they pay out a large portion of their earnings as dividends instead of reinvesting them into expanding their business. Dividend stocks may also face competition from newer and more innovative companies that can disrupt their market share and profitability. Dividend stocks may lag behind the market performance in periods of economic expansion and optimism.

3. **High Valuation:** Dividend stocks can become overvalued if they attract too much demand from investors who are seeking income and stability. A high valuation can reduce the dividend yield and the margin of safety of dividend stocks and increase the risk of a price correction if the market sentiment changes or the company fails to meet expectations. High valuation can also limit the upside potential of dividend stocks, as they may have reached their fair value or become overpriced.

Chapter 2

Building a Strong Foundation

This chapter will teach you how to lay a solid foundation for your investment journey. You will discover how to assess your financial goals and risk tolerance, which will help you align your investment strategy with your individual circumstances. You will also learn how to create a well-defined investment plan that takes into account the need for diversification and risk management. Finally, you will learn how to understand dividends and dividend yield, which will empower you to make informed decisions.

Assessing Your Financial Goals and Risk Tolerance

One of the first steps in your investment journey is to assess your financial goals and risk tolerance. This will help you determine why you are investing, what you are investing for, and how much risk you are willing to take. Having clear and realistic financial goals and risk tolerance will help you align your investment strategy with your individual circumstances and avoid unnecessary stress and disappointment.

Financial goals are the specific outcomes that you want to achieve with your money. They can vary depending on your personal situation, preferences, and values. Some common financial goals are:

1. **Saving for Retirement**: This is the goal of accumulating enough money to support your desired lifestyle after you stop working. Retirement planning involves estimating how much income you will need, how long you will live, and how much you can save and invest.

2. **Buying a House**: This is the goal of purchasing a property that meets your needs and preferences. Buying a house involves saving for a down payment, securing a mortgage, and paying for maintenance and taxes.

3. **Funding Education**: This is the goal of paying for your own or your children's education expenses. Education planning involves estimating the cost of tuition, fees, books, and living expenses, as well as applying for scholarships, grants, and loans.

To make your financial goals more effective and achievable, you should use the SMART criteria. SMART stands for Specific, Measurable, Achievable, Relevant, and Time-bound. Here is how to apply the SMART criteria to your financial goals:

1. **Specific**: Your financial goals should be clear and well-defined. You should state exactly what you want to accomplish, how much money you need, and why it is important to you. For

example, instead of saying, "I want to save for retirement," you should say, "I want to save $1 million by age 65 so that I can retire comfortably".

2. **Measurable:** Your financial goals should be quantifiable and trackable. You should be able to measure your progress and success by using numbers and indicators. For example, instead of saying, "I want to buy a house," you should say, "I want to buy a 3-bedroom house for $300,000 in 5 years".

3. **Achievable:** Your financial goals should be realistic and attainable. You should consider your current situation, resources, and constraints when setting your financial goals. You should also break down your financial goals into smaller and manageable steps. For example, instead of saying, "I want to fund my child's education," you should say, "I want to save $50,000 for my child's college tuition in 10 years by investing $300 per month".

4. **Relevant:** Your financial goals should be meaningful and aligned with your values and priorities. You should focus on the financial goals that matter most to you and that will have the most impact on your life. You should also avoid conflicting or competing financial goals that may distract or derail you from your main objectives. For example, instead of saying, "I want to travel the world," you should say, "I want to travel to Europe for 2 weeks next year as a reward for achieving my career goal".

5. **Time-Bound:** Your financial goals should have a specific deadline or timeframe. You should set a clear start date and end date for your financial goals. This will help you create a sense of urgency and motivation. It will also help you monitor your performance and adjust your plan if needed. For example, instead of saying, "I want to pay off my debt," you should say, "I want to pay off my $10,000 credit card debt in 2 years by paying $500 per month".

Risk tolerance is the degree of uncertainty or volatility that you are willing or able to accept when investing. Risk tolerance can affect your investment decisions, returns, and emotions. Understanding your risk tolerance will help you choose an investment strategy that matches your personality and comfort level.

Risk tolerance can vary depending on several factors, such as:

1. **Age:** Your age can influence your risk tolerance because it affects your time horizon and life stage. Generally, younger investors have a longer time horizon and can afford to take more risk because they have more time to recover from losses. Older investors have a shorter time horizon and may prefer less risk because they have less time to make up for losses.

2. **Income:** Your income can influence your risk tolerance because it affects your ability to save and invest. Generally, higher-income investors have more disposable income and can afford to take more risks because they have more money to invest. Lower-income investors have less disposable income and may prefer less risk because they have less money to invest.

3. **Expenses:** Your expenses can influence your risk tolerance because they affect your cash flow and liquidity. Generally, lower-expense investors have more cash flow and liquidity and can afford to take more risk because they have more money available for investing. Higher-expense investors have less cash flow and liquidity and may prefer less risk because they have less money available for investing.

4. **Assets:** Your assets can influence your risk tolerance because they affect your net worth and diversification. Generally, higher-asset investors have more net worth and diversification and can afford to take more risk because they have more wealth and security. Lower-asset investors have less net worth and diversification and may prefer less risk because they have less wealth and security.

5. **Liabilities:** Your liabilities can influence your risk tolerance because they affect your debt and leverage. Generally, lower-liability investors have less debt and leverage and can afford to take more risk because they have less financial obligations and pressure. Higher-liability investors have more debt and leverage and may prefer less risk because they have more financial obligations and pressure.

6. **Personality:** Your personality can influence your risk tolerance because it affects your preferences and emotions. Generally, more adventurous and optimistic investors have higher risk tolerance because they enjoy taking challenges and opportunities. More cautious and pessimistic investors have lower risk tolerance because they avoid taking risks and uncertainties.

Based on these factors, you can classify your risk tolerance into three main categories:

1. **Conservative:** You have a low-risk tolerance and prefer to preserve your capital and avoid losses. You are willing to accept lower returns in exchange for higher safety and stability. You are suitable for low-risk investments, such as bonds, money market funds, or CDs.

2. **Moderate:** You have a medium risk tolerance and prefer to balance your capital growth and income. You are willing to accept moderate returns in exchange for moderate risk and volatility. You are suitable for medium-risk investments, such as dividend stocks, balanced funds, or REITs.

3. **Aggressive:** You have a high-risk tolerance and prefer to maximize your capital growth and returns. You are willing to accept higher risk and volatility in exchange for higher potential returns. You are suitable for high-risk investments, such as growth stocks, sector funds, or options.

To assess your financial goals and risk tolerance, you can use various tools and methods, such as:

1. **Online Calculators:** You can use online calculators to estimate your financial goals and risk tolerance by inputting your information and answering some questions. For example, you

can use the Financial Goals Calculator to calculate how much you need to save and invest for your financial goals. You can also use the Risk Tolerance Quiz to determine your risk profile based on your answers.

2. **Financial Advisors**: You can consult with a financial advisor to help you assess your financial goals and risk tolerance by providing you with professional advice and guidance. A financial advisor can help you create a personalized investment plan that suits your needs and preferences. You can find a qualified financial advisor by using the Financial Advisor Finder tool.

3. **Self-Assessment**: You can conduct a self-assessment to evaluate your financial goals and risk tolerance by using your own judgment and experience. A self-assessment can help you reflect on your personal situation, preferences, and values. You can use the SMART Criteria Worksheet to write down your financial goals using the SMART criteria. You can also use the Risk Tolerance Scale to rate your risk tolerance level based on different scenarios.

Assessing your financial goals and risk tolerance is an essential step in your investment journey. It will help you define your purpose, direction, and strategy for investing. It will also help you avoid unnecessary stress and disappointment by choosing investments that match your personality and comfort level. By following the tips and resources provided in this section, you can effectively assess your financial goals and risk tolerance.

Creating a Well-Defined Investment Plan

After you have assessed your financial goals and risk tolerance, the next step in your investment journey is to create a well-defined investment plan. An investment plan is a document that outlines your investment strategy and actions. It helps you stay focused, disciplined, and consistent with your investment decisions. It also helps you avoid emotional and impulsive trading, which can harm your returns and increase your risk.

An investment plan should align with your financial goals and risk tolerance. It should reflect your personal situation, preferences, and values. It should also be flexible and adaptable to changing market conditions and circumstances.

You can choose from many different investment strategies, depending on your investment objectives, horizon, and style. Some of the most common investment strategies are:

1. **Value Investing:** This is the strategy of buying stocks that are undervalued by the market based on their intrinsic value. Value investors look for companies that have strong fundamentals, such as earnings, cash flow, assets, or dividends, but are trading at a discount to their true worth. Value investors believe that the market will eventually recognize the value of these stocks and reward them with higher prices.

2. **Growth Investing:** This is the strategy of buying stocks that have a high potential for growth in their earnings and revenues. Growth investors look for innovative, disruptive, or dominant companies in their industries. Growth investors believe that these companies will continue to grow faster than the market and generate higher returns.

3. **Dividend Investing:** This is the strategy of buying stocks that pay dividends to their shareholders regularly. Dividend investors look for companies with stable and sustainable dividend policies and dividend growth potential. Dividend investors believe that dividends provide a steady source of income and capital appreciation.

To choose an investment strategy that suits your needs and preferences, you should consider the following factors:

- **Your Investment Objective:** What are you trying to achieve with your investment? Are you looking for income, growth, or both?

- **Your Investment Horizon:** How long do you plan to hold your investment? Are you investing for the short-term, medium-term, or long-term?

- **Your Risk Tolerance:** How much risk are you willing or able to take with your investment? Are you comfortable with high volatility, low liquidity, or high leverage?

- **Your Investment Style:** What kind of investor are you? Are you more analytical or intuitive? Are you more active or passive? Are you more conservative or aggressive?

You can choose an investment strategy that matches your profile based on these factors. For example, if you are looking for income and have a low-risk tolerance and a long-term horizon, you may prefer dividend investing. You may prefer growth investing if you are looking for growth and have a high-risk tolerance and a short-term horizon. If you are looking for both income and growth and have a moderate risk tolerance and a medium-term horizon, you may prefer value investing.

Once you have chosen an investment strategy, you should create an investment plan that includes the following elements:

1. **Investment Objective:** This is the statement of what you want to accomplish with your investment. It should be clear, specific, measurable, achievable, relevant, and time-bound. For example, "I want to save $100,000 for my retirement in 20 years by investing $500 per month in dividend stocks".

2. **Investment Horizon:** This is the timeframe of how long you plan to hold your investment. It should be realistic and consistent with your financial goals and life stage. For example, "I plan to hold my investment for 20 years until I retire at age 65".

3. **Asset Allocation:** This is the division of your portfolio among different asset classes, such as stocks, bonds, or cash. It should be based on your risk tolerance and expected returns. For example, "I allocate 80% of my portfolio to stocks and 20% to bonds".

4. **Security Selection:** This is the process of choosing individual securities within each asset class. It should be based on your investment strategy and criteria. For example, "I select dividend stocks that have a dividend yield of at least 4%, a dividend payout ratio of less than 60%, and a dividend growth rate of at least 10%".

5. **Portfolio Rebalancing:** This is the adjustment of your portfolio to maintain your desired asset allocation. It should be done periodically or when there are significant changes in the market or your circumstances. For example, "I rebalance my portfolio every year or when my asset allocation deviates by more than 5% from my target".

Diversifying and Managing Risk

Diversifying and managing risk are two essential aspects of investing that can help you achieve your financial goals and avoid unnecessary losses. In this section, you will learn why it is important to diversify your portfolio and manage risk when investing. You will also learn how to diversify your portfolio and manage risk by using various methods and techniques.

Diversification is the practice of spreading your investments across different asset classes, sectors, industries, countries, and companies. Diversification can reduce the overall risk of your portfolio by minimizing the impact of any single or specific risk factor. For example, if you invest all your money in one stock, you are exposed to the risk of that stock losing value due to company-specific issues, such as poor earnings, lawsuits, or scandals. However, if you invest your money in a diversified portfolio of stocks from different sectors and industries, you are less likely to suffer a large loss due to any single company's problems.

Types of Risk and Diversification

Many types of risk can affect your investments, such as:

1. **Market Risk:** This is the risk of losing money due to changes in the overall market conditions, such as interest rates, inflation, economic growth, or political events. Market risk affects all investments to some degree, but some are more sensitive than others. For example, bonds are more affected by interest rate changes than stocks.

2. **Company Risk:** This is the risk of losing money due to issues related to a specific company or industry, such as earnings, management, competition, regulation, or innovation. Company risk affects only the investments related to that company or industry but not the rest of the market. For example, a pharmaceutical company's stock may drop due to a failed drug trial or a patent expiration.

3. **Inflation Risk:** This is the risk of losing purchasing power due to the increase in the general level of prices over time. Inflation risk affects all investments, but some are more vulnerable

than others. For example, cash and fixed-income investments are more eroded by inflation than stocks or real estate.

4. **Currency Risk**: This is the risk of losing money due to changes in the exchange rate between different currencies. Currency risk affects only the investments denominated in foreign currencies but not the domestic ones. For example, a U.S. investor who owns a European stock may lose money if the euro depreciates against the dollar.

Diversification can help you reduce these types of risks by creating a balanced portfolio that can withstand various market scenarios and conditions. However, diversification does not eliminate all risks. There is still a possibility that your entire portfolio may lose value due to a systemic or catastrophic event that affects the whole market or economy. Therefore, diversification should be combined with other methods of risk management.

To measure the diversification of your portfolio, you can use metrics such as correlation and standard deviation. Correlation is a measure of how closely two investments move together in the same direction. Correlation ranges from -1 to 1, where -1 means perfect negative correlation (moving in opposite directions), 0 means no correlation (moving independently), and 1 means perfect positive correlation (moving in the same direction). A diversified portfolio should have a low or negative correlation among its components, meaning they do not move in sync. For example, if one investment goes up while another goes down, they can offset each other's losses and gains.

Standard deviation is a measure of how much an investment's returns vary from its average over time. Standard deviation indicates how volatile or risky an investment is. A higher standard deviation means higher volatility and higher risk. A lower standard deviation means lower volatility and lower risk. A diversified portfolio should have a lower standard deviation than its individual components, which means that it has less variation and less risk.

To manage the risk of your portfolio, you can use techniques such as stop-loss orders, hedging, or insurance. Stop-loss orders are instructions to sell an investment when it reaches a certain price level or percentage loss. Stop-loss orders can help you limit your losses and protect your profits by automatically exiting a position when it goes against your expectations. For example, if you buy a stock at $50 and set a stop-loss order at $45, you will sell the stock if it drops below $45.

Hedging is the practice of using one investment to offset the risk of another investment. Hedging can help you reduce your exposure to a specific type of risk by taking an opposite position in a related investment. For example, if you own a stock that is sensitive to interest rate changes, you can hedge your interest rate risk by buying a bond that benefits from interest rate changes.

Insurance is the practice of paying a fee or premium to transfer the risk of a loss to another party. Insurance can help you protect your portfolio from unforeseen events that may cause large losses or damages. For example, if you own a house that is vulnerable to fire or flood damage, you can buy an insurance policy that covers the cost of repairing or replacing your house in case of such disasters.

Understanding Dividends and Dividend Yield

Dividends are payments that companies make to distribute a portion of their earnings to their shareholders. Dividends are one of the ways that investors can earn income from their stock investments. Dividends also indicate the financial health and profitability of a company.

Types of Dividends

There are different types of dividends that companies can pay to their shareholders, such as:

1. **Regular Dividends:** These are dividends that are paid on a regular and consistent basis, such as quarterly, semi-annually, or annually. Regular dividends are usually based on a fixed amount or a percentage of the company's earnings per share. For example, Coca-Cola pays a regular quarterly dividend of $0.42 per share.

2. **Special Dividends**: These are dividends that are paid on an occasional or one-time basis, usually as a result of a windfall or an extraordinary event. Special dividends are usually larger than regular dividends and are not expected to be repeated. For example, Microsoft paid a special dividend of $3 per share in 2004.

3. **Stock Dividends:** These are dividends that are paid in the form of additional shares of stock instead of cash. Stock dividends increase the number of shares owned by the shareholders but do not change the total value of their holdings. Stock dividends are usually expressed as a percentage or a ratio of the existing shares. For example, Apple issued a 4-for-1 stock dividend in 2020, which means that each shareholder received four shares for every share they owned.

The companies pay dividends to their shareholders on a specific date, known as the payment date. However, not all shareholders are eligible to receive the dividends. Only the shareholders who own the shares before a certain date, known as the ex-dividend date, are entitled to the dividends. The ex-dividend date is usually one or two days before the record date, which is the date when the company determines who are the shareholders of record. The record date is usually two or three weeks before the payment date.

Dividends and Taxes

Dividends are taxed differently depending on the type and source of the dividends and the shareholder's tax status and location. Generally, there are two types of dividends for tax purposes:

1. **Qualified Dividends:** These are dividends that meet certain criteria, such as being paid by a U.S. corporation or a foreign corporation that is eligible for tax treaty benefits. Qualified dividends are taxed at a lower rate than ordinary income, which can range from 0% to 20%, depending on the shareholder's tax bracket.

2. **Ordinary Dividends:** These are dividends that do not meet the criteria for qualified dividends, such as being paid by a REIT or an MLP. Ordinary dividends are taxed at the same rate as ordinary income, ranging from 10% to 37%, depending on the shareholder's tax bracket.

The dividend yield is a measure of how much income an investor can expect to receive from a dividend stock. The dividend yield is calculated by dividing the annual dividend per share by the current share price. The dividend yield is expressed as a percentage and indicates the return on investment from dividends alone.

For example, if a company pays $1 in dividends per year and its share price is $20, its dividend yield is 5% ($1/$20). This means that an investor buying this stock at $20 will receive $1 in dividends per year for each share they own, equivalent to 5% of their initial investment.

Dividend yield can be used to compare the attractiveness and performance of different dividend stocks and sectors. Generally, a higher dividend yield means a higher income and a lower valuation for a stock. However, a higher dividend yield may also indicate a higher risk or a lower growth potential for a stock. Therefore, dividend yield should not be used in isolation but in conjunction with other factors, such as dividend payout ratio, dividend growth rate, earnings growth rate, and price-to-earnings ratio.

Chapter 3

Identifying High-Quality Dividend Stocks

In this chapter, you will learn how to identify high-quality dividend stocks that can provide you with income and growth. You will discover how to research and evaluate dividend stocks by using various tools and techniques. You will also learn how to combine fundamental and technical analysis to make well-reasoned choices in your stock selections.

Researching Dividend Stocks

Research is crucial in dividend stock trading because it helps you find and select the best dividend stocks that can meet your investment goals and risk tolerance. Research also helps you avoid investing in low-quality or risky dividend stocks that may cut or eliminate their dividends or lose their value.

Research Sources

There are many sources and methods of research that you can use to find and analyze dividend stocks, such as:

1. **Financial Statements**: These are documents that provide information about a company's financial performance and position, such as income statements, balance sheets, and cash flow statements. Financial statements can help you assess a company's earnings, revenue, cash flow, debt, and profitability, which are important indicators of its financial health and stability.

2. **Analyst Reports:** These are reports that provide opinions and recommendations from experts or professionals who follow and evaluate a company or an industry. Analyst reports can help you get insights and perspectives on a company's strengths, weaknesses, opportunities, and threats, as well as its future prospects and growth potential.

3. **News Articles**: These are articles that provide information and updates on a company or an industry, such as events, trends, developments, or announcements. News articles can help you stay informed and aware of the factors that may affect a company's performance and dividend policy, such as market conditions, competition, regulation, or innovation.

4. **Online Tools:** These are tools that provide data and analysis on a company or an industry, such as stock screeners, dividend calculators, or charts. Online tools can help you filter and

compare dividend stocks based on various criteria and metrics, such as dividend yield, dividend payout ratio, dividend growth rate, or dividend history.

To assess a company's financial health and stability, you can use indicators such as:

1. **Earnings**: This is the amount of money that a company makes after deducting its expenses. Earnings indicate how profitable and efficient a company is. A company with high and consistent earnings can afford to pay and increase its dividends over time. A company with low or negative earnings may struggle to maintain or grow its dividends.

2. **Revenue**: This is the amount of money that a company receives from selling its products or services. Revenue indicates how popular and competitive a company is. A company with high and growing revenue can generate more earnings and cash flow to support its dividends. A company with low or declining revenue may face challenges in sustaining or raising its dividends.

3. **Cash flow**: This is the amount of money that a company generates and spends on its operations. Cash flow indicates how liquid and solvent a company is. A company with high and positive cash flow can easily cover its dividends and other obligations. A company with low or negative cash flow may have difficulties in paying its dividends and debts.

4. **Debt**: This is the amount of money that a company owes to its creditors. Debt indicates how leveraged and risky a company is. A company with low or manageable debt can have more financial flexibility and stability to pay its dividends. A company with high or excessive debt may have more financial pressure and uncertainty to pay its dividends.

5. **Profitability**: This is the ratio of a company's earnings to its revenue. Profitability indicates how efficient and productive a company is. A company with high and improving profitability can have more margins and returns to pay its dividends. A company with low or deteriorating profitability may have less margins and returns to pay its dividends.

To assess a company's dividend policy and history, you can use indicators such as:

1. **Dividend Yield:** This is the ratio of the annual dividend per share to the current share price. Dividend yield measures how much income an investor can expect to receive from a dividend stock. A higher dividend yield means a higher income and a lower valuation for a stock. However, a higher dividend yield may also indicate a higher risk or a lower growth potential for a stock.

2. **Dividend Payout Ratio:** This is the percentage of a company's earnings that it pays out as dividends. The dividend payout ratio indicates how sustainable and stable a company's dividend policy is. A lower dividend payout ratio means that a company retains more earnings for reinvestment and growth, which can support future dividends. A higher dividend payout ratio means that a company distributes more earnings to shareholders, which can limit future dividends.

3. **Dividend Growth Rate**: This is the annual percentage increase in a company's dividend per share. The dividend growth rate reflects how much a company is willing and able to raise its dividends over time. A higher dividend growth rate means that a company has strong earnings growth and confidence in its future prospects, which can enhance shareholder value. A lower dividend growth rate means that a company has weak earnings growth or uncertainty in its future prospects, which can reduce shareholder value.

4. **Dividend History**: This is the record of how long and how often a company has paid dividends to its shareholders. Dividend history shows how consistent and reliable a company's dividend policy is. A longer and uninterrupted dividend history means that a company has a proven track record of paying dividends through various market cycles and conditions. A shorter or interrupted dividend history means that a company has a less established track record of paying dividends or has cut or eliminated its dividends in the past.

Evaluating Dividend Stocks

To evaluate a company's dividend quality and performance, you can use criteria such as consistency, reliability, sustainability, or growth potential. These criteria can help you determine how likely a company is to continue paying and increasing its dividends in the future.

1. **Consistency:** This is the degree to which a company pays dividends on a regular and predictable basis. A consistent dividend payer shows that it has a stable and disciplined dividend policy that does not change with market conditions or earnings fluctuations. A consistent dividend payer also shows that it has a loyal and satisfied shareholder base that expects and values its dividends. For example, Coca-Cola has paid dividends consistently since 1893 and has increased its dividends for 59 consecutive years.

2. **Reliability:** This is the degree to which a company pays dividends without interruption or reduction. A reliable dividend payer shows that it has a strong and resilient financial position that can withstand economic downturns and external shocks. A reliable dividend payer also shows that it has a high priority and commitment to rewarding its shareholders with dividends. For example, Procter & Gamble has paid dividends reliably since 1890 and has never cut or suspended its dividends.

3. **Sustainability**: This is the degree to which a company pays dividends that are supported by its earnings and cash flow. A sustainable dividend payer shows that it has a profitable and efficient business model that can generate enough earnings and cash flow to cover its dividends and other obligations. A sustainable dividend payer also shows that it has a prudent and conservative dividend payout ratio that leaves room for reinvestment and growth. For example, Microsoft has paid dividends sustainably since 2003 and has maintained a dividend payout ratio of less than 40%.

4. **Growth Potential**: This is the degree to which a company pays dividends that can increase over time. A growth dividend payer shows that it has a dynamic and innovative business strategy that can grow its earnings and cash flow at a faster rate than the market. A growth dividend payer also shows that it has a generous and progressive dividend growth rate that reflects its confidence and optimism in its future prospects. For example, Apple has paid dividends with growth potential since 2012 and has increased its dividends by an average of 10% per year.

Comparing and Ranking Dividend Stocks

To compare and rank dividend stocks based on their attractiveness and suitability for your investment goals and risk tolerance, you can use metrics such as:

1. **Dividend Yield:** This is the ratio of the annual dividend per share to the current share price. Dividend yield measures how much income an investor can expect to receive from a dividend stock. A higher dividend yield means a higher income and a lower valuation for a stock. However, a higher dividend yield may also indicate a higher risk or a lower growth potential for a stock.

2. **Dividend Payout Ratio:** This is the percentage of a company's earnings that it pays out as dividends. The dividend payout ratio indicates how sustainable and stable a company's dividend policy is. A lower dividend payout ratio means that a company retains more earnings for reinvestment and growth, which can support future dividends. A higher dividend payout ratio means that a company distributes more earnings to shareholders, which can limit future dividends.

3. **Dividend Growth Rate:** This is the annual percentage increase in a company's dividend per share. The dividend growth rate reflects how much a company is willing and able to raise its dividends over time. A higher dividend growth rate means that a company has strong earnings growth and confidence in its future prospects, which can enhance shareholder value. A lower dividend growth rate means that a company has weak earnings growth or uncertainty in its future prospects, which can reduce shareholder value.

4. **Total Return:** This is the combination of capital appreciation and dividend income from an investment. Total return measures how much an investor can earn from a dividend stock over time. A higher total return means a higher return on investment and a higher compounding effect from reinvesting dividends. A lower total return means a lower return on investment and a lower compounding effect from reinvesting dividends.

Based on these metrics, you can compare and rank dividend stocks by using online tools such as Dividend Stock Screener or Dividend Stock Ranker. These tools can help you filter, sort, and rank dividend stocks based on various criteria and metrics, such as dividend yield, dividend payout ratio, dividend growth rate, or total return. You can also customize your own criteria and metrics according to your investment goals and risk tolerance.

For example, if you are looking for high-income dividend stocks with low risk, you may use the following criteria:

- Dividend yield: Above 4%

- Dividend payout ratio: Below 60%

- Dividend growth rate: Above 5%

- Total return: Above 10%

Using these criteria, you may find some high-quality dividend stocks from different sectors and industries, such as:

Stock	Sector	Industry	Dividend Yield	Dividend Payout Ratio	Dividend Growth Rate	Total Return
AT&T	Communicaton Services	Telecom Services	6.8%	58%	6%	13%
Chevron	Energy	Oil & Gas	5.2%	54%	7%	12%
Johnson & Johnson	Health Care	Pharmace uticals	4.1%	49%	8%	12%
Realty Income	Real Estate	REITs	4.3%	57%	5%	11%
Verizon	Communication Services	Telecom Services	4.4%	48%	5%	10%

These are some examples of how to evaluate, compare, and rank dividend stocks based on their dividend quality and performance. You can use these methods and techniques to find and select the best dividend stocks that can meet your investment goals and risk tolerance.

Combining Fundamental and Technical Analysis

Fundamental and technical analysis are two different approaches to analyzing and evaluating stocks. They differ in their methods, assumptions, and applications.

Fundamental analysis is the approach of studying the intrinsic value of a stock based on its financial performance, competitive advantage, growth potential, and future prospects. Fundamental analysis uses tools and techniques such as valuation ratios, financial statements, analyst reports, or news articles. Fundamental analysis assumes that the market price of a stock will eventually reflect its true value and that investors can profit by buying undervalued stocks or selling overvalued stocks.

Technical analysis is the approach of studying the price movements and patterns of a stock based on its historical data, market trends, and investor behavior. Technical analysis uses tools and techniques such as trend lines, moving averages, indicators, or charts. Technical analysis assumes that the market price of a stock is determined by the forces of supply and demand and that investors can profit by following the prevailing market direction or anticipating future price changes.

To make well-reasoned choices in your stock selections, you can combine fundamental and technical analysis to get a more complete and balanced picture of a stock. You can use fundamental analysis to identify high-quality dividend stocks that have strong financial health and stability, consistent and reliable dividend payments, and sustainable growth potential. You can use technical analysis to determine the optimal timing and price to buy or sell these dividend stocks based on their price trends, patterns, signals, and levels.

For example, suppose you are interested in buying a dividend stock from the technology sector. You can use fundamental analysis to screen for dividend stocks that have a high dividend yield, a low dividend payout ratio, a high dividend growth rate, and a high earnings growth rate. You may find some candidates, such as Microsoft, Apple, or Cisco. You can then use technical analysis to compare their price charts and look for indicators such as:

1. **Entry Point:** This is the price level at which you can buy a stock at a favorable or discounted price. An entry point can be identified by using tools such as support levels, trend lines, moving averages, or oversold indicators. For example, you may find an entry point for Microsoft when its price bounces off its 200-day moving average or when its RSI indicator falls below 30.

2. **Exit Point:** This is the price level at which you can sell a stock at a profitable or premium price. An exit point can be identified by using tools such as resistance levels, trend lines, moving averages, or overbought indicators. For example, you may find an exit point for Apple when its price breaks above its 52-week high or when its MACD indicator crosses above its signal line.

3. **Buy Signal:** This is a sign that indicates that the price of a stock is likely to increase shortly. A buy signal can be generated by using tools such as bullish patterns, breakouts, crossovers, or divergences. For example, you may get a buy signal for Cisco when its price forms an ascending triangle pattern or when its stochastic indicator diverges from its price.

4. **Sell Signal:** This is a sign that indicates that the price of a stock is likely to decrease shortly. A sell signal can be generated by using tools such as bearish patterns, breakdowns, crossovers, or divergences. For example, you may get a sell signal for Microsoft when its price forms a double-top pattern or when its volume indicator diverges from its price.

By combining fundamental and technical analysis, you can make more informed and rational decisions in your stock selections.

Common Mistakes

Some common mistakes to avoid when combining fundamental and technical analysis are:

1. Relying on only one type of analysis and ignoring the other. Both fundamental and technical analysis can provide valuable insights and perspectives on a stock, and using them together can help you get a more complete and balanced picture. For example, fundamental analysis can help you identify high-quality dividend stocks that have strong financial health and stability, consistent and reliable dividend payments, and sustainable growth potential. Technical analysis can help you determine the optimal timing and price to buy or sell these dividend stocks based on their price trends, patterns, signals, and levels.

2. Confusing correlation with causation. Correlation is a measure of how closely two variables move together, while causation is a relationship where one variable causes or affects another. Just because two variables are correlated does not mean that one causes the other or vice versa. For example, just because a stock's price moves in sync with its earnings does not mean that the earnings cause the price movements or that the price movements affect the earnings. There may be other factors or variables that influence both the earnings and the price, such as market conditions, competition, or innovation.

3. Overlooking the context and limitations of each type of analysis. Fundamental and technical analysis have different assumptions, methods, and applications, and each has its own strengths and weaknesses. You should be aware of the context and limitations of each type of analysis and use them appropriately. For example, fundamental analysis may not be very useful for short-term trading, as it takes time for the market to reflect the true value of a stock. Technical analysis may not be very reliable for long-term investing as it does not account for the underlying value or quality of a stock.

4. Ignoring your own investment goals and risk tolerance. Ultimately, your investment decisions should be based on your own investment goals and risk tolerance, not on what others say or do. You should use fundamental and technical analysis as tools to help you make informed and rational choices, not as rules to follow blindly. You should also be flexible and adaptable to changing market conditions and circumstances and adjust your strategy accordingly. For example, if your goal is to generate income from dividends, you

should focus on dividend yield, dividend payout ratio, dividend growth rate, and total return1. If your goal is to achieve capital appreciation from price movements, you should focus on trend lines, moving averages, indicators, and charts.

Chapter 4

The Power of Dividend Reinvestment

In this chapter, you will learn about the power of dividend reinvestment and how it can help you accelerate your wealth accumulation and achieve your financial goals. You will discover what dividend reinvestment plans (DRIPs) are and how they work. You will also learn how to set up and manage a DRIP portfolio effectively and how to deal with the tax implications and considerations of dividend reinvestment.

What Are Dividend Reinvestment Plans (DRIPs)?

Dividend reinvestment plans (DRIPs) are programs that allow you to automatically reinvest your dividends into more shares of the same stock instead of receiving them as cash. DRIPs can help you increase your ownership and compound your returns over time.

Types of DRIPs

There are different types of DRIPs that you can choose from, depending on the provider and the features, such as:

1. **Full DRIPs**: These are DRIPs that are offered by the companies themselves, usually through a transfer agent or a registrar. Full DRIPs allow you to buy and reinvest shares directly from the company without paying any commissions or fees. Full DRIPs may also offer discounts, fractional shares, or optional cash purchases.

2. **Partial DRIPs:** These are DRIPs that are offered by some brokers or online platforms. Partial DRIPs allow you to reinvest only a portion of your dividends into more shares of the same stock while receiving the rest as cash. Partial DRIPs may also offer flexibility, convenience, or diversification.

3. **Synthetic DRIPs**: These are DRIPs that are offered by some brokers or online platforms. Synthetic DRIPs allow you to reinvest your dividends into more shares of the same stock, but not directly from the company. Synthetic DRIPs may use the market price or the closing price to buy the shares and may charge commissions or fees.

Advantages and Disadvantages

The advantages and disadvantages of DRIPs compared to other methods of investing dividends, such as cash dividends or dividend stocks, are:

Advantages:

1. DRIPs can help you save time and money by automating your dividend reinvestment and avoiding commissions or fees.

2. DRIPs can help you benefit from compounding and dollar-cost averaging by increasing your share count and lowering your average cost per share over time.

3. DRIPs can help you grow your portfolio and income faster by reinvesting your dividends at a higher rate than the market or inflation.

Disadvantages:

1. DRIPs can increase your tax liability and complexity by generating taxable income and capital gains, even if you do not receive any cash.

2. DRIPs can reduce your liquidity and flexibility by locking up your dividends and making it harder to access or use your cash for other purposes.

3. DRIPs can expose you to more risk and volatility by concentrating your portfolio and income on one stock or sector.

Set Up and Manage a DRIP Portfolio Effectively

To set up and manage a DRIP portfolio effectively, you can follow these steps:

1. **Choose a Suitable DRIP Provider:** Depending on your preferences and needs, you can choose a DRIP provider that offers the features and services that you want. For example, if you want to buy and reinvest shares directly from the company, you can choose a full DRIP provider, such as a transfer agent or a registrar. If you want to have more flexibility and convenience, you can choose a partial or synthetic DRIP provider, such as a broker or an online platform. You can compare and review different DRIP providers by using online tools such as DRIP Investor or DRIP Wizard.

2. **Select High-Quality Dividend Stocks:** Once you have chosen a DRIP provider, you can select the dividend stocks that you want to buy and reinvest in your DRIP portfolio. You should look for high-quality dividend stocks that have strong financial health and stability, consistent and reliable dividend payments, and sustainable growth potential. You can use criteria such as dividend yield, dividend payout ratio, dividend growth rate, or total return

to screen and rank dividend stocks. You can also use online tools such as Dividend Stock Screener or Dividend Stock Ranker to filter and compare dividend stocks based on various criteria and metrics.

3. **Monitor and Evaluate Your DRIP Portfolio Performance:** After you have set up your DRIP portfolio, you should monitor and evaluate its performance regularly. You should track the changes in your share count, dividend income, and portfolio value over time. You should also measure the returns and risk of your DRIP portfolio by using metrics such as compound annual growth rate (CAGR), internal rate of return (IRR), or time-weighted return (TWR). You can use online tools such as DRIP Calculator or DRIP Performance Tracker to calculate and visualize your DRIP portfolio performance.

4. **Optimize and Diversify Your DRIP Portfolio:** To improve your DRIP portfolio performance and reduce your risk, you should optimize and diversify your DRIP portfolio periodically. You should adjust your portfolio allocation according to your investment goals and risk tolerance. You should also diversify your portfolio across different asset classes, sectors, industries, countries, and companies. You can use techniques such as dollar-cost averaging (DCA), value averaging (VA), or asset allocation to optimize and diversify your DRIP portfolio. You can also use online tools such as Portfolio Analyzer or Portfolio Optimizer to analyze and optimize your DRIP portfolio.

Dealing with the Tax Implications and Considerations of Dividend Reinvestment

One of the challenges of dividend reinvestment is dealing with the tax implications and considerations that may arise from it. Dividend reinvestment can affect your tax liability and reporting in different ways, depending on the type and source of the dividends and your tax status and location. In this section, you will learn how dividends and capital gains are taxed differently, how DRIPs can affect your tax liability and reporting, and how to minimize your tax burden and maximize your returns from DRIPs.

Dividends and capital gains are two types of income that you can earn from your stock investments. Dividends are payments that companies make to distribute a portion of their earnings to their shareholders. Capital gains are profits that you make from selling your stocks at a higher price than you bought them. Dividends and capital gains are taxed differently depending on the type and source of the dividends and your tax status and location.

1. **Type of Dividends:** Generally, there are two types of dividends for tax purposes: qualified dividends and ordinary dividends. Qualified dividends are dividends that meet certain criteria, such as being paid by a U.S. corporation or a foreign corporation that is eligible for tax treaty benefits. Qualified dividends are taxed at a lower rate than ordinary income, which can range from 0% to 20%, depending on your tax bracket. Ordinary dividends are

dividends that do not meet the criteria for qualified dividends, such as being paid by a REIT or an MLP. Ordinary dividends are taxed at the same rate as ordinary income, which can range from 10% to 37%, depending on your tax bracket.

2. **Source of Dividends:** The source of dividends refers to the country or jurisdiction where the company that pays the dividends is located or incorporated. The source of dividends can affect your tax liability depending on whether you are a resident or a nonresident of that country or jurisdiction. For example, if you are a U.S. resident who receives dividends from a U.S. company, you will pay U.S. taxes on those dividends according to your tax bracket and type of dividends. However, if you are a U.S. resident who receives dividends from a foreign company, you may also pay foreign taxes on those dividends according to the foreign country's tax laws and treaties. You may be able to claim a foreign tax credit or deduction to avoid double taxation on those dividends.

3. **Tax Status and Location**: Your tax status and location refer to your personal situation and circumstances that may affect your tax liability and reporting. Your tax status and location can include factors such as your filing status, income level, deductions, credits, exemptions, or residency. For example, if you are married and file jointly with your spouse, you may have a higher income threshold and lower tax rate than if you file separately or single. If you have a low income or qualify for certain deductions or credits, you may pay no or minimal taxes on your dividends or capital gains. If you live in a state or city that has no or low-income taxes, you may save more on your taxes than if you live in a state or city that has high-income taxes.

DRIPs can affect your tax liability and reporting in different ways, depending on whether you reinvest your dividends before or after taxes.

1. **Before-Tax DRIPs:** These are DRIPs that allow you to reinvest your dividends without paying any taxes on them until you sell your shares. Before-tax DRIPs are usually offered by the companies themselves through full DRIPs. Before-tax DRIPs can help you defer your taxes and compound your returns over time by increasing your share count and cost basis. However, before-tax DRIPs can also increase your tax complexity and reporting by requiring you to keep track of your dividend income, reinvestment dates, share prices, and cost basis for each purchase.

2. **After-Tax DRIPs**: These are DRIPs that require you to pay taxes on your dividends before reinvesting them into more shares. After-tax DRIPs are usually offered by brokers or online platforms through partial or synthetic DRIPs. After-tax DRIPs can help you simplify your taxes and reporting by allowing you to report your dividend income and pay taxes on it in the same year. However, after-tax DRIPs can also reduce your returns over time by decreasing your share count and cost basis.

Strategies to Minimize Tax

To minimize your tax burden and maximize your returns from DRIPs, you can use strategies such as:

1. **Holding Your DRIP Stocks in a Tax-Advantaged Account**: A tax-advantaged account is an account that offers special tax benefits for investing purposes, such as an IRA, a 401(k), or a Roth IRA. A tax-advantaged account can help you reduce or eliminate your taxes on your dividends and capital gains by allowing you to defer or exempt them from taxation until withdrawal or distribution. However, a tax-advantaged account may also have limitations or restrictions on contributions, withdrawals, distributions, or investments.

2. **Choosing Qualified Dividends Over Ordinary Dividends:** Qualified dividends are taxed at a lower rate than ordinary income, while ordinary dividends are taxed at the same rate as ordinary income. Therefore, choosing qualified dividends over ordinary dividends can help you save on your taxes and increase your returns. However, not all dividends are qualified, and you may have to meet certain requirements or criteria to qualify for them.

3. **Harvesting Your Tax Losses:** Tax loss harvesting is the practice of selling your losing stocks to offset your gains from your winning stocks, thereby reducing your taxable income and capital gains. Tax loss harvesting can help you lower your taxes and increase your returns by allowing you to use your losses to your advantage. However, tax loss harvesting may also have drawbacks or risks, such as triggering the wash sale rule, missing out on future gains, or increasing your trading costs.

Chapter 5

Crafting Your Dividend Stock Trading Strategy

In this chapter, you will learn how to craft your own dividend stock trading strategy that suits your investment goals and risk tolerance. You will discover how to choose between income-focused and growth-oriented trading approaches, define entry and exit criteria for your investments, compare long-term and short-term trading strategies, and incorporate market trends and economic indicators into your decision-making process.

Income-Focused vs. Growth-Oriented Trading Approaches

The difference between income-focused and growth-oriented trading approaches is that income-focused trading aims to generate steady and consistent income from dividends, while growth-oriented trading aims to achieve capital appreciation from price movements.

Income-focused trading is suitable for investors who are looking for income stability, cash flow, or passive income. Income-focused traders tend to invest in high-yield, low-growth dividend stocks that pay regular and reliable dividends. Income-focused traders also tend to hold their stocks for a long time and reinvest their dividends to compound their returns. Income-focused trading can provide a hedge against inflation, market volatility, or economic downturns.

Growth-oriented trading is suitable for investors who are looking for capital preservation, wealth accumulation, or active income. Growth-oriented traders tend to invest in low-yield, high-growth dividend stocks that have strong earnings growth and dividend growth potential. Growth-oriented traders also tend to trade their stocks more frequently and take advantage of price fluctuations. Growth-oriented trading can provide higher returns, a higher compounding effect, or higher liquidity.

Examples:

Some examples of income-focused and growth-oriented dividend stocks are:

1. **Income-Focused Dividend Stocks**: These are stocks that pay high and consistent dividends but have low or moderate growth potential. Income-focused dividend stocks are suitable for investors who are looking for income stability, cash flow, or passive income. Some examples of income-focused dividend stocks are:

   • **AT&T Inc. (T):** This is a telecom giant that offers wireless, broadband, video, and media services. AT&T has a dividend yield of 8.16% as of Oct. 22, 2021, which is one of the highest among the S&P 500 companies. AT&T has also raised its dividend for 37 consecutive years, making it a Dividend Aristocrat. However, AT&T faces fierce competition, regulatory pressure, and high debt levels, which may limit its growth prospects.

- **Chevron Corp. (CVX):** This is an energy major that engages in oil and gas exploration, production, refining, and marketing. Chevron has a dividend yield of 5.2% as of Aug. 28, 20213, which is above the industry average. Chevron has also increased its dividend for 34 consecutive years, making it another Dividend Aristocrat2. However, Chevron is exposed to the volatility and uncertainty of oil and gas prices, which may affect its earnings and cash flow.

- **Kimberly-Clark Corp. (KMB):** This is a consumer goods company that produces and sells personal care, tissue, and paper products. Kimberly-Clark has a dividend yield of 3.7% as of Aug. 28, 20213, which is higher than the sector average. Kimberly-Clark has also boosted its dividend for 49 consecutive years, making it one of the longest-running Dividend Aristocrats. However, Kimberly-Clark faces rising costs, intense competition, and changing consumer preferences, which may hamper its growth potential.

2. **Growth-Oriented Dividend Stocks:** These are stocks that pay low or moderate dividends but have high or above-average growth potential. Growth-oriented dividend stocks are suitable for investors who are looking for capital preservation, wealth accumulation, or active income. Some examples of growth-oriented dividend stocks are:

- **Apple Inc. (AAPL):** This is a technology giant that designs, manufactures, and sells consumer electronics, software, and online services. Apple has a dividend yield of 0.6% as of Aug. 28, 2021, which is below the market average. However, Apple has a dividend growth rate of 10% per year as of July 16, 2021, which is well above the market average. Apple also has a strong brand loyalty, innovation capability, and cash position, which can support its future growth and dividends.

- **Broadcom Inc. (AVGO):** This is a semiconductor company that provides chips and software solutions for various industries and applications. Broadcom has a dividend yield of 3% as of Aug. 28, 2021, which is in line with the industry average. However, Broadcom has a dividend growth rate of 51% per year as of July 16, 2021, which is one of the highest among the S&P 500 companies. Broadcom also has a diversified product portfolio, a loyal customer base, and a robust acquisition strategy, which can fuel its growth and dividends.

- **Prologis Inc. (PLD):** This is a real estate investment trust (REIT) that owns and operates industrial properties such as warehouses and distribution centers. Prologis has a dividend yield of 2% as of Aug. 28, 2021, which is lower than the REIT average. However, Prologis has a dividend growth rate of 9% per year as of July 16, 2021, which is higher than the REIT average. Prologis also benefits from the rising demand for e-commerce logistics, the limited supply of industrial space, and the global diversification of its portfolio.

Pros and Cons of Each Approach

Here are some of the pros and cons of each approach:

1. **Income-Focused Trading**: This approach aims to generate a steady stream of income from investments that pay dividends, interest, or rents. Some examples of income-focused investments are bonds, dividend stocks, real estate investment trusts (REITs), and annuities.

- **Pros:** Income-focused trading can provide a reliable source of passive income that can supplement other sources of income or fund living expenses. Income-focused investments tend to be less volatile than growth-oriented investments, as they are less affected by market fluctuations and economic cycles. Income-focused trading can also reduce portfolio risk by diversifying the sources of returns and providing a cushion against capital losses.

- **Cons:** Income-focused trading may have lower returns than growth-oriented trading in the long run, as income-focused investments tend to have lower capital appreciation potential. Income-focused trading may also expose investors to inflation risk, as the income payments may lose purchasing power over time. Income-focused trading may also have higher tax implications, as income payments are usually taxed at ordinary income rates.

2. **Growth-Oriented Trading:** This approach aims to increase the value of investments by investing in companies or sectors that have high growth potential. Some examples of growth-oriented investments are growth stocks, technology stocks, biotechnology stocks, and emerging markets stocks.

- **Pros:** Growth-oriented trading can provide impressive returns in the short term, as growth-oriented investments can benefit from positive market sentiment, innovation, and competitive advantages. Growth-oriented trading can also increase the value of the portfolio over time, as growth-oriented investments can compound their returns and reinvest their earnings. Growth-oriented trading can also offer tax advantages, as capital gains are usually taxed at lower rates than income payments.

- **Cons:** Growth-oriented trading may have a higher risk than income-focused trading, as growth-oriented investments tend to be more volatile and sensitive to market conditions and economic cycles. Growth-oriented trading may also require more research and analysis, as growth-oriented investments may have complex business models, uncertain future prospects, and high valuations. Growth-oriented trading may also have lower or no income payments, as growth-oriented investments tend to reinvest their earnings rather than pay dividends.

Defining Entry and Exit Criteria for Your Investments

Entry and exit criteria are the rules or conditions that you use to decide when to enter and exit a trade. They are important for your trading strategy because they can help you achieve your trading objectives, manage your risk, and improve your performance.

Entry criteria are the factors that you consider before opening a position in the market. They can be based on technical analysis, fundamental analysis, market sentiment, or a combination of these. Some examples of entry criteria are:

- A specific price level or pattern that indicates a potential trend reversal or continuation.

- A specific indicator value or signal that confirms a trading opportunity.

- A specific news event or economic data release that affects the market direction or volatility.

- A specific risk/reward ratio that meets your risk tolerance and profit expectation.

Exit criteria are the factors that you consider before closing a position in the market. They can be based on the same factors as entry criteria or different ones depending on your trading style and goals. Some examples of exit criteria are:

- A specific price level or pattern that indicates potential trend exhaustion or reversal.

- A specific indicator value or signal that warns of a possible market change or divergence.

- A specific news event or economic data release that contradicts your trading hypothesis or increases your risk exposure.

- A specific profit/loss level or percentage that satisfies your trading plan or triggers your stop-loss order.

By defining clear entry and exit criteria for your investments, you can:

- Increase your chances of entering the market at the right time and direction.

- Increase your chances of exiting the market at the right time and price.

- Reduce your emotional stress and bias when making trading decisions.

- Evaluate your trading performance and improve your trading skills.

Examples

1. **Price:** This is the most basic factor that determines when to buy or sell a stock. You can use different price levels or patterns to identify entry and exit points. For example, you can use support and resistance levels, trend lines, moving averages, Fibonacci retracements, or candlestick patterns to find potential entry and exit points based on price action.

2. **Dividend Yield**: This is the ratio of the annual dividend per share to the current share price. It measures how much income you can get from holding a stock. You can use dividend yield as an entry or exit criterion based on your income objectives and risk tolerance. For example, you can buy a stock when its dividend yield is high compared to its historical average or its peers, indicating that it is undervalued or offers a high return. You can sell a stock when its dividend yield is low compared to its historical average or its peers, indicating that it is overvalued or offers a low-income return.

3. **Dividend Growth Rate:** This is the annual percentage change in the dividend per share. It measures how much the company increases its dividend payments over time. You can use the dividend growth rate as an entry or exit criterion based on your growth objectives and risk tolerance. For example, you can buy a stock when its dividend growth rate is high compared to its historical average or its peers, indicating that it has strong earnings growth and shareholder value creation. You can sell a stock when its dividend growth rate is low compared to its historical average or its peers, indicating that it has weak earnings growth and shareholder value creation.

4. **Valuation Ratio**: This is the ratio of the stock price to some measure of the company's value, such as earnings, sales, book value, or cash flow. It measures how expensive or cheap a stock is relative to its fundamentals. You can use the valuation ratio as an entry or exit criterion based on your value objectives and risk tolerance. For example, you can buy a stock when its valuation ratio is low compared to its historical average or its peers, indicating that it is undervalued or offers a margin of safety. You can sell a stock when its valuation ratio is high compared to its historical average or its peers, indicating that it is overvalued or offers a margin of error.

5. **Technical Indicator:** This is a mathematical calculation based on the price, volume, or other data of a stock. It generates signals that indicate the direction, strength, momentum, trend, volatility, or sentiment of the market. You can use technical indicators as an entry or exit criterion based on your technical objectives and risk tolerance. For example, you can buy a stock when its technical indicator gives a bullish signal, such as crossing above a certain level, moving above a certain line, forming a certain pattern, or diverging from the price. You can sell a stock when its technical indicator gives a bearish signal, such as crossing below a certain level, moving below a certain line, forming a certain pattern, or converging with the price.

Aligning your entry and exit criteria with your financial goals is a crucial step in developing a successful trading strategy. Here are some general guidelines on how to do that, based on some common financial goals:

1. **Income Generation:** If your goal is to generate a steady stream of income from your investments, you may want to use entry and exit criteria that focus on dividend yield, dividend growth rate, interest rate, or cash flow. For example, you may enter a trade when

the dividend yield of a stock is above a certain threshold, indicating that it offers a high-income return. You may exit a trade when the dividend growth rate of a stock falls below a certain level, indicating that it has weak earnings growth and shareholder value creation. You may also use technical indicators that measure the strength and direction of the trend, such as moving averages or trend lines, to confirm your entry and exit signals.

2. **Capital Preservation**: If your goal is to protect your principal and avoid large losses, you may want to use entry and exit criteria that focus on risk management, volatility, and valuation. For example, you may enter a trade when the risk/reward ratio of an investment is favorable, indicating that it offers a margin of safety. You may exit a trade when the volatility of an investment increases beyond your risk tolerance, indicating that it exposes you to more uncertainty and potential loss. You may also use technical indicators that measure the momentum and divergence of the market, such as relative strength index (RSI) or moving average convergence divergence (MACD), to warn you of possible market changes or reversals.

3. **Wealth Accumulation:** If your goal is to increase the value of your portfolio over time, you may want to use entry and exit criteria that focus on capital appreciation, growth potential, and innovation. For example, you may enter a trade when the valuation ratio of a stock is low compared to its historical average or its peers, indicating that it is undervalued or offers a margin of error. You may exit a trade when the valuation ratio of a stock is high compared to its historical average or its peers, indicating that it is overvalued or offers a margin of error. You may also use technical indicators that measure the sentiment and breakout of the market, such as Bollinger bands or stochastic oscillators, to identify trading opportunities or trends.

Long-Term vs Short-Term Trading Strategies

Long-term and short-term trading strategies are two different approaches to investing in the financial markets, such as stocks, forex, commodities, or cryptocurrencies. They differ in terms of their time horizon, risk-reward profile, trading frequency, and methods of analysis. Here are some of the main differences between long-term and short-term trading strategies:

1. **Time Horizon**: Long-term trading strategies involve holding an asset for a year or more, while short-term trading strategies involve holding an asset for a year or less or even just a few weeks or days for some traders. Long-term traders aim to capture the long-term trends and growth potential of an asset, while short-term traders aim to exploit the short-term fluctuations and volatility of an asset.

2. **Risk-Reward Profile**: Long-term trading strategies tend to have lower risk and lower returns than short-term trading strategies, as they are less affected by market noise and temporary price movements. Long-term traders also incur lower transaction costs and taxes as they

trade less frequently and benefit from lower capital gains rates. Short-term trading strategies tend to have higher risk and higher returns than long-term trading strategies, as they are more exposed to market uncertainty and sudden price changes. Short-term traders also incur higher transaction costs and taxes as they trade more frequently and pay higher income tax rates.

3. **Trading Frequency**: Long-term trading strategies involve fewer trades and longer holding periods than short-term trading strategies, as they require less monitoring and adjustment of the positions. Long-term traders may only trade a few times a year or even less, depending on their investment objectives and market conditions. Short-term trading strategies involve more trades and shorter holding periods than long-term trading strategies, as they require more attention and reaction to the market movements. Short-term traders may trade several times a day or even more, depending on their trading style and market opportunities.

4. **Methods of Analysis**: Long-term trading strategies rely more on fundamental analysis than short-term trading strategies, as they focus on the intrinsic value and future prospects of an asset. Long-term traders use financial statements, economic indicators, industry trends, and other qualitative factors to evaluate an asset's performance and potential. Short-term trading strategies rely more on technical analysis than long-term trading strategies, as they focus on the price action and patterns of an asset. Short-term traders use charts, indicators, signals, and other quantitative tools to identify entry and exit points for an asset.

Examples

1. **Buy-and-Hold**: This is a long-term trading strategy that involves buying an asset and holding it for a long time, regardless of the market fluctuations. The objective of this strategy is to benefit from the long-term growth potential and compounding effect of an asset. The method of analysis for this strategy is mainly fundamental, as it focuses on the intrinsic value and future prospects of an asset. Some examples of assets that are suitable for this strategy are blue-chip stocks, index funds, or cryptocurrencies.

2. **Dividend Growth Investing**: This is a long-term trading strategy that involves buying and holding stocks that pay regular and increasing dividends over time. The objective of this strategy is to generate a steady and growing stream of income from the dividends, as well as capital appreciation from the stock price. The method of analysis for this strategy is mainly fundamental, as it focuses on the financial strength, earnings growth, and dividend policy of the companies. Some examples of stocks that are suitable for this strategy are dividend aristocrats, dividend kings, or dividend champions.

3. **Swing Trading**: This is a short-term trading strategy that involves buying and selling an asset within a few days or weeks based on the price swings or cycles of the market. The objective of this strategy is to exploit the short-term fluctuations and volatility of an asset.

The method of analysis for this strategy is mainly technical, as it focuses on the price action and patterns of an asset. Some examples of assets that are suitable for this strategy are stocks, forex, commodities, or cryptocurrencies.

Each of the trading strategies mentioned above has its own advantages and disadvantages, depending on your trading objectives, risk tolerance, and personal preferences. Here are some of the pros and cons of each strategy:

Buy-and-Hold: This strategy has the following advantages and disadvantages:

Advantages:

1. It can provide long-term returns that match or exceed the market performance, as it benefits from the long-term growth potential and the compounding effect of an asset.

2. It can reduce the risk of losing money due to market noise and temporary price movements, as it ignores the short-term fluctuations and volatility of an asset.

3. It can lower transaction costs and taxes, as it trades less frequently and benefits from lower capital gains rates.

4. It can save time and effort, as it requires less monitoring and adjustment of the positions.

Disadvantages:

1. It may miss out on some short-term opportunities or trends that could generate higher returns, as it does not exploit the short-term fluctuations and volatility of an asset.

2. It may expose the portfolio to systemic risk or market crashes, as it does not hedge or diversify the positions.

3. It may require a large initial investment and a long time horizon, as it needs to overcome the opportunity cost and inflation effects of holding an asset for a long time.

4. It may be affected by behavioral biases or emotions, such as overconfidence, anchoring, or loss aversion, that could impair the decision-making process.

Dividend Growth Investing: This strategy has the following advantages and disadvantages:

Advantages:

1. It can generate a steady and growing stream of income from the dividends, as well as capital appreciation from the stock price, that could enhance the total return of the portfolio.

2. It can invest in high-quality companies that have strong financial strength, earnings growth, and shareholder value creation that could increase the stability and performance of the portfolio.

3. It can benefit from the dividend reinvestment plan (DRIP), which allows reinvesting the dividends into more shares of the same company, which could accelerate the compounding effect and growth potential of the portfolio.

4. It can reduce the risk of dividend cuts or suspensions, as it focuses on companies that have a consistent and sustainable dividend policy that could protect the income stream and portfolio value.

Disadvantages:

1. It may have lower returns than other growth-oriented strategies, as it invests in mature and stable companies that have lower growth potential than emerging or innovative companies.

2. It may expose the portfolio to sector or industry risk, as it tends to concentrate on certain sectors or industries that have higher dividend payouts than others, such as utilities, consumer staples, or financials.

3. It may incur higher taxes than other capital appreciation strategies, as it pays taxes on the dividends at ordinary income rates rather than capital gains rates.

4. It may be affected by market conditions or economic cycles, as it depends on the profitability and cash flow of the companies to maintain or increase their dividends.

Swing Trading: This strategy has the following advantages and disadvantages:

Advantages:

1. It can provide impressive returns in a short period, as it exploits the short-term fluctuations and volatility of an asset.

2. It can trade in any market direction or condition, as it can profit from both rising and falling markets by going long or short on an asset.

3. It can use leverage or margin to amplify the returns or losses of an asset, as it borrows money from a broker to trade with more capital than is available in the account.

4. It can use various technical tools and methods to identify entry and exit points for an asset, such as charts, indicators, signals, and patterns.

Disadvantages:

1. It may have a higher risk than other trading strategies, as it exposes the portfolio to market uncertainty and sudden price changes.

2. It may incur higher transaction costs and taxes than other trading strategies, as it trades more frequently and pays higher income tax rates.

3. It may require more time and attention than other trading strategies, as it needs to monitor and react to market movements constantly.

4. It may be affected by psychological factors or emotions, such as greed, fear, stress, or frustration, that could influence trading behavior.

Incorporating Market Trends and Economic Indicators into Your Decision-Making Process

Market trends and economic indicators are two important factors that can affect your trading performance. Here are some explanations and examples of what they are and how they can influence your trading decisions:

1. **Market Trends:** These are the general directions or movements of the prices of an asset, a sector, or a market over time. They can be classified as bullish, bearish, or sideways, depending on whether the prices are rising, falling, or moving within a range. They can also be categorized as long-term, medium-term, or short-term, depending on their duration and magnitude. Some examples of market trends are:

- **Bull Market**: This is a market trend that is characterized by rising prices and increasing investor confidence. It usually occurs when the economy is growing, the earnings are improving, and the sentiment is optimistic. A bull market can last for months or years, depending on the underlying factors and conditions. For example, the U.S. stock market experienced a bull market from March 2009 to February 2020, when the S&P 500 index rose from 676.53 to 3,386.15 points, an increase of over 400%.

- **Bear Market**: This is a market trend that is characterized by falling prices and decreasing investor confidence. It usually occurs when the economy is contracting, the earnings are deteriorating, and the sentiment is pessimistic. A bear market can last for weeks or months, depending on the severity and extent of the decline. For example, the U.S. stock market experienced a bear market from February 2020 to March 2020, when the S&P 500 index dropped from 3,386.15 to 2,237.40 points, a decrease of over 33%.

- **Sideways Market**: This is a market trend that is characterized by fluctuating prices and mixed investor confidence. It usually occurs when the economy is stable, the earnings are consistent, and the sentiment is neutral. A sideways market can last for days or weeks, depending on the balance and range of the movements. For example, the U.S. stock market experienced a sideways market from April 2020 to May 2020, when the S&P 500 index moved between 2,237.40 and 2,955.45 points, a variation of about 32%.

2. **Economic Indicators**: These are specific macroeconomic statistics that can be used to understand and predict the state and direction of the economy. They can be classified as leading, lagging, or coincident, depending on whether they precede, follow, or coincide with

the economic cycles. They can also be categorized as domestic or international, depending on whether they reflect the conditions of a single country or a group of countries. Some examples of economic indicators are:

- **Gross Domestic Product (GDP):** This is a coincident economic indicator that measures the total value of all goods and services produced within a country during a given period. It reflects the size and growth of the economy and its various sectors. It also affects the income and spending of consumers and businesses. For example, in 2020, the U.S. GDP contracted by 3.5%, its worst performance since 1946. This indicated that the U.S. economy suffered a severe recession due to the COVID-19 pandemic.

- **Unemployment Rate**: This is a lagging economic indicator that measures the percentage of people in the labor force who are actively looking for work but cannot find it. It reflects the availability and quality of jobs and the level of economic activity. It also affects the consumption and saving of households and the production and investment of firms. For example, in April 2020, the U.S. unemployment rate surged to 14.8%, its highest level since 1948. This indicated that the U.S. labor market faced a massive shock due to the COVID-19 lockdowns.

- **Consumer Price Index (CPI):** This is a lagging economic indicator that measures the changes in the prices of a basket of goods and services that are typically purchased by consumers. It reflects the inflation rate and the purchasing power of money. It also affects the interest rates and exchange rates of currencies and bonds. For example, in March 2021, the U.S. CPI increased by 2.6% year-over-year. This indicated that the U.S. inflation rate accelerated due to higher energy prices and base effects.

How to incorporate market trends and economic indicators into your decision-making process:

Market trends and economic indicators can help you make better trading decisions by providing you with valuable information about where the prices of an asset, a sector, or a market are heading and why they are moving in that direction.

You can use market trends to identify trading opportunities or threats based on your trading objectives, style, and time horizon. For example:

1. If you are a long-term investor who wants to achieve capital appreciation over time, you may want to buy and hold an asset that is in a long-term bullish trend, as it indicates that the asset has strong growth potential and positive momentum. You may also want to avoid or sell an asset that is in a long-term bearish trend, as it indicates that the asset has weak growth potential and negative momentum.

2. If you are a short-term trader who wants to exploit price fluctuations over time, you may want to buy and sell an asset that is in a short-term bullish or bearish trend, as it indicates that the asset has high volatility and clear direction. You may also want to avoid or trade

sideways an asset that is in a sideways trend, as it indicates that the asset has low volatility and mixed direction.

You can use economic indicators to analyze the fundamental factors and conditions that affect the prices of an asset, a sector, or a market. For example:

1. If you are trading stocks, you may want to use GDP, unemployment rate, and CPI to assess the health and outlook of the economy and its various sectors. You may also want to use earnings, dividends, and valuation ratios to evaluate the performance and potential of individual companies.

2. If you are trading forex, you may want to use interest rates, exchange rates, and trade balance to measure the strengths and weaknesses of different currencies and their relative values. You may also want to use political events, monetary policies, and market sentiment to anticipate the changes and movements of currency pairs.

You can incorporate market trends and economic indicators into your decision-making process by adjusting your portfolio allocation, diversification, and risk management according to your analysis and expectations. For example:

1. If you expect a long-term bullish trend for an asset, a sector, or a market based on positive economic indicators, you may want to increase your exposure or allocation to that asset, sector, or market in your portfolio. You may also want to reduce your diversification or correlation with other assets, sectors, or markets that have negative economic indicators or opposite trends.

2. If you expect a short-term bearish trend for an asset, a sector, or a market based on negative economic indicators, you may want to decrease your exposure or allocation to that asset, sector, or market in your portfolio. You may also want to increase your diversification or correlation with other assets, sectors, or markets that have positive economic indicators or opposite trends.

3. If you are uncertain about the direction or duration of a trend for an asset, a sector, or a market based on mixed or conflicting economic indicators, you may want to maintain your exposure or allocation to that asset, sector, or market in your portfolio. You may also want to balance your diversification or correlation with other assets, sectors, or markets that have similar or different economic indicators or trends.

4. In any case, you should always manage your risk by using appropriate tools and techniques such as stop-loss orders, trailing stops, hedging strategies, position sizing, leverage control, and risk-reward ratio.

Chapter 6

Mitigating Risks in Dividend Stock Trading

Risk management is crucial in any investment endeavor, especially in dividend stock trading, where investors seek to generate consistent income from their holdings. Dividend stocks are shares of companies that pay out a portion of their earnings to shareholders regularly, usually quarterly or annually. Dividend stocks can offer investors several benefits, such as stable cash flow, capital appreciation, tax advantages, and protection against inflation. However, dividend stocks are not risk-free, and investors need to be aware of the potential pitfalls and challenges that may arise in this type of investment. This is what you are going to learn in this chapter.

Market Volatility and Dividend Stocks

Market volatility is the degree of variation in the prices of stocks or other assets over time. It is often measured by indicators such as the VIX index, beta, and standard deviation. Market volatility can have a significant impact on dividend stocks, which are shares of companies that pay out a portion of their earnings to shareholders regularly.

One of the impacts of market volatility on dividend stocks is price fluctuations. Dividend stocks tend to be less volatile than non-dividend stocks, as they offer investors a stable and predictable income stream. However, dividend stocks are not immune to market swings, and their prices can rise or fall depending on various factors, such as earnings, interest rates, inflation, economic conditions, and investor sentiment. For example, dividend stocks may suffer during periods of rising interest rates, as investors may shift their preferences to fixed-income securities that offer higher yields. Conversely, dividend stocks may benefit during periods of falling interest rates, as investors may seek out alternative sources of income that can protect them against inflation.

Another impact of market volatility on dividend stocks is dividend cuts. Dividend cuts are reductions in the amount or frequency of dividend payments by a company. Dividend cuts can occur for various reasons, such as declining earnings, cash flow problems, debt obligations, strategic changes, or regulatory issues. Dividend cuts can harm dividend stocks, as they signal a deterioration in the company's financial health and performance. Dividend cuts can also erode investor confidence and trust in the company, leading to lower demand and lower prices for its shares. For example, during the COVID-19 pandemic in 2020, many companies across different sectors and industries announced dividend cuts or suspensions to preserve cash and cope with the economic downturn. This resulted in a sharp decline in the value of many dividend stocks.

A third impact of market volatility on dividend stocks is capital losses. Capital losses are decreases in the value of an investment below its purchase price. Capital losses can occur when investors sell their shares at a lower price than what they paid for them or when they hold on to their shares while their prices fall below their cost basis. Capital losses can affect dividend stocks during periods of high market volatility, as investors may panic and sell their shares to avoid further losses or as investors may face margin calls or liquidity issues that force them to liquidate their positions. Capital losses can offset or outweigh the income received from dividends, resulting in a negative total return for dividend stock investors.

In summary, market volatility can have a significant impact on dividend stocks, such as price fluctuations, dividend cuts, and capital losses. Dividend stock investors need to be aware of these risks and adopt appropriate strategies to mitigate them and protect their portfolios during market downturns. Some of these strategies include hedging, diversification, and fundamental analysis, which you will learn in the following sections.

Measuring Market Volatility

Market volatility can be measured by indicators such as the VIX index, beta, and standard deviation. These indicators can help investors assess the level of risk and uncertainty in the market and in their dividend stocks.

1. The VIX index, also known as the fear index, is a measure of the expected volatility of the S&P 500 index over the next 30 days. It is calculated based on the prices of options on the S&P 500 index. A high VIX index indicates that investors expect large price movements in the market, while a low VIX index indicates that investors expect calm and stable market conditions. The VIX index can help investors gauge the overall market sentiment and mood and adjust their portfolio accordingly. For example, during the COVID-19 pandemic in 2020, the VIX index reached a record high of 82.69 on March 16, reflecting the extreme fear and panic in the market.

2. Beta is a measure of the sensitivity of a stock's price to the movements of the market or a benchmark index. It is calculated based on the historical correlation and covariance between the stock and the market or index. A beta of 1 means that the stock moves in sync with the market or index, while a beta greater than 1 means that the stock is more volatile than the market or index, and a beta less than 1 means that the stock is less volatile than the market or index. Beta can help investors evaluate the systematic risk or market risk of a stock and choose stocks that match their risk tolerance and investment objectives. For example, a conservative investor may prefer low-beta dividend stocks that offer stable returns and lower risk, while an aggressive investor may prefer high-beta dividend stocks that offer higher returns and higher risk.

3. Standard deviation is a measure of the dispersion or variability of a stock's price or returns over time. It is calculated based on the average deviation from the mean or expected value of the price or returns. A high standard deviation indicates that the stock's price or returns are widely spread out and unpredictable, while a low standard deviation indicates that the stock's price or returns are closely clustered around the mean and predictable. Standard deviation can help investors measure the unsystematic risk or specific risk of a stock and assess its performance relative to its historical average or benchmark. For example, a dividend stock with a high standard deviation may have a higher potential for capital gains or losses, while a dividend stock with a low standard deviation may have a lower potential for capital gains or losses.

Pros and Cons

Investing in high-volatility and low-volatility dividend stocks has its pros and cons, and investors need to balance risk and reward in different market conditions.

High-volatility dividend stocks are dividend stocks that have high beta, high standard deviation, or both. They tend to be more sensitive to market fluctuations and company-specific news and may experience larger price swings than low-volatility dividend stocks. Some examples of high-volatility dividend stocks are energy stocks, technology stocks, biotechnology stocks, etc.

- **Pros:** High-volatility dividend stocks can offer higher returns than low-volatility dividend stocks in favorable market conditions, as they can capture more upside potential from positive market trends or company events. They can also provide higher dividend yields than low-volatility dividend stocks, as they tend to have lower prices relative to their dividends.

- **Cons:** High-volatility dividend stocks can also incur higher losses than low-volatility dividend stocks in unfavorable market conditions, as they can suffer more downside risk from negative market trends or company events. They can also have lower dividend safety than low-volatility dividend stocks, as they may be more likely to cut or suspend their dividends due to financial distress or operational challenges.

Low-volatility dividend stocks are dividend stocks that have low beta, low standard deviation, or both. They tend to be less sensitive to market fluctuations and company-specific news and may experience smaller price swings than high-volatility dividend stocks. Some examples of low-volatility dividend stocks are utility stocks, consumer staples stocks, healthcare stocks, etc.

- **Pros**: Low-volatility dividend stocks can offer lower losses than high-volatility dividend stocks in unfavorable market conditions, as they can cushion more downside risk from negative market trends or company events. They can also provide higher dividend safety than high-volatility dividend stocks, as they may be less likely to cut or suspend their dividends due to financial stability or operational resilience.

- **Cons:** Low-volatility dividend stocks can also offer lower returns than high-volatility dividend stocks in favorable market conditions, as they can capture less upside potential from positive market trends or company events. They can also provide lower dividend yields than high-volatility dividend stocks, as they tend to have higher prices relative to their dividends.

To balance risk and reward in different market conditions, investors need to consider their risk tolerance, investment horizon, income needs, and portfolio objectives when choosing between high-volatility and low-volatility dividend stocks. They also need to monitor the market volatility indicators and adjust their portfolio allocation accordingly. For example, they may increase their exposure to high-volatility dividend stocks when the market is calm and bullish and decrease their exposure to high-volatility dividend stocks when the market is volatile and bearish. They may also use a combination of high-volatility and low-volatility dividend stocks to create a diversified and balanced portfolio that can generate consistent income and capital appreciation over time.

Hedging Strategies for Dividend Stocks

Hedging is a strategy that involves taking a position in an asset or a derivative that can offset the potential losses or gains of another investment. Hedging can help investors protect their portfolios during market downturns, especially if they hold dividend stocks that may be affected by price fluctuations, dividend cuts, or capital losses. However, hedging is not a risk-free or cost-free strategy, and you need to be careful not to over-hedge your portfolio, as it can reduce your returns and increase costs.

Options

Options are contracts that give the buyer the right, but not the obligation, to buy or sell an underlying asset at a specified price and date. Options can be used to hedge dividend stocks by buying put options or selling call options on the same or similar stocks. A put option gives the buyer the right to sell the underlying asset at a predetermined price, while a call option gives the buyer the right to buy the underlying asset at a predetermined price. For example, suppose an investor owns 100 shares of ABC, a dividend-paying stock that trades at $50 per share. The investor expects to receive a $1 dividend per share on the ex-dividend date but is also concerned about the stock price dropping after the dividend payment. To hedge against this risk, the investor can buy a put option on ABC with a strike price of $49 and an expiration date after the ex-dividend date. This way, if ABC drops below $49 after the dividend payment, the investor can exercise the put option and sell ABC at $49, thus locking in a profit of $1 per share (the dividend minus the difference between the strike price and the stock price). However, if ABC stays above $49 after the dividend payment, the investor can let the put option expire worthless and keep ABC and the dividend. The cost of buying the put option is the premium paid to the option seller, which reduces the net return of the hedging strategy. Alternatively, the investor can sell a call option on ABC with a strike price of $51 and an expiration date after the ex-dividend date. This way, if ABC rises above $51 after the dividend payment, the investor can deliver ABC at $51 to the option buyer, thus locking in a profit of $2 per share (the difference between the strike price and the stock price plus the dividend). However, if ABC stays below $51 after the dividend payment, the investor can keep ABC and the dividend. The benefit of selling the call option is the premium received from the option buyer, which increases the net return of the hedging strategy. However, selling a call option also limits the upside potential of ABC and exposes the investor to unlimited losses if ABC rises significantly above $51.

1. **Benefits:** Options can provide flexible and customized hedging strategies for dividend stocks, as investors can choose different strike prices and expiration dates to suit their risk-reward preferences. Options can also generate income from premiums or dividends while reducing downside risk or limiting upside potential.

2. **Drawbacks:** Options can be expensive and complex to trade, as they involve paying or receiving premiums, commissions, and fees. Options can also expire worthless or out-of-the-money, resulting in losses or missed opportunities. Options can also be affected by factors such as volatility, time decay, and interest rates, which can change their value and profitability.

3. **Best Scenarios:** Options are best suited for hedging dividend stocks when investors have a specific view of the direction and magnitude of the stock price movement after the dividend payment. Options are also best suited for hedging dividend stocks when investors want to generate income from premiums or dividends while reducing downside risk or limiting upside potential.

Inverse ETFs

Inverse ETFs are exchange-traded funds that track the opposite performance of an underlying index or asset class. Inverse ETFs can be used to hedge dividend stocks by buying inverse ETFs that track the same or similar sectors, industries, or markets as their dividend stocks. For example, suppose an investor owns a portfolio of dividend stocks that track the S&P 500 index, which is a broad-based index of 500 large-cap US companies. The investor is concerned about a possible market downturn that may affect the value and performance of their dividend stocks. To hedge against this risk, the investor can buy an inverse ETF that tracks the inverse performance of the S&P 500 index, such as the ProShares Short S&P 500 ETF (SH). This way, if the S&P 500 index drops by 10%, the inverse ETF will rise by 10%, thus offsetting the losses from the dividend stocks. However, if the S&P 500 index rises by 10%, the inverse ETF will drop by 10%, thus reducing the gains from the dividend stocks. The cost of buying the inverse ETF is the expense ratio, which is the annual fee charged by the fund manager to cover the operational costs of the fund.

1. **Benefits:** Inverse ETFs can provide simple and convenient hedging strategies for dividend stocks, as investors can buy inverse ETFs that track the same or similar sectors, industries, or markets as their dividend stocks. Inverse ETFs can also provide diversified and broad-based exposure to different segments of the market and reduce the risk of picking individual stocks or options.

2. **Drawbacks:** Inverse ETFs can be risky and complex to trade, as they involve using leverage, derivatives, and short-selling techniques to achieve their inverse performance. Inverse ETFs can also suffer from tracking errors, which occur when the inverse ETF does not match the exact opposite performance of its underlying index or asset class. Inverse ETFs can also be affected by factors such as compounding, rebalancing, and liquidity, which can change their value and profitability over time.

3. **Best Scenarios:** Inverse ETFs are best suited for hedging dividend stocks when investors have a general view of the direction and magnitude of the market or sector movement that may affect their dividend stocks. Inverse ETFs are also best suited for hedging dividend stocks when investors want to hedge their entire portfolio or a large portion of it with a single or a few inverse ETFs.

Gold

Gold is a precious metal that is widely regarded as a safe-haven asset and a store of value. Gold can be used to hedge dividend stocks by buying physical gold or gold-related securities, such as gold coins, bars, futures, options, ETFs, or mining stocks. For example, suppose an investor owns a portfolio of dividend stocks that are exposed to various risks, such as inflation, currency devaluation, geopolitical tensions, or economic recessions. To hedge against these risks, the investor can buy physical gold or gold-related securities that can preserve their purchasing power and wealth in times of uncertainty and crisis. This way, if these risks materialize and affect the value and performance of their dividend stocks, the investor can benefit from the increase in the price and demand of gold. However, if these risks do not materialize and their dividend stocks perform well, the investor may miss out on some of the gains from their dividend stocks due to the opportunity cost of holding gold. The cost of buying gold or gold-related securities depends on various factors, such as supply and demand, production costs, storage costs, transaction costs, etc.

1. **Benefits**: Gold can provide a reliable and long-term hedging strategy for dividend stocks, as gold has historically maintained its value and purchasing power over time and across different economic cycles. Gold can also provide protection against various risks that may affect dividend stocks, such as inflation, currency devaluation, geopolitical tensions, or economic recessions.

2. **Drawbacks:** Gold can be expensive and inconvenient to buy and store, as it involves paying for transportation, storage, insurance, taxes, commissions, etc. Gold can also be volatile and unpredictable in its price movements, as it is influenced by various factors beyond its

intrinsic value, such as speculation, sentiment, expectations, etc. Gold can also have low or negative returns in periods of low inflation or high economic growth.

3. **Best Scenarios:** Gold is best suited for hedging dividend stocks when investors have a long-term view of the preservation of their wealth and purchasing power in times of uncertainty and crisis. Gold is also best suited for hedging dividend stocks when investors want to hedge against various risks that may affect their dividend stocks beyond market fluctuations.

The importance of hedging only a portion of their portfolio and not over-hedging cannot be overstated. Hedging is a trade-off between risk and return. By hedging their portfolio with options, inverse ETFs, or gold, investors can reduce their exposure to market fluctuations and other risks that may affect their dividend stocks. However, by hedging their portfolio with options, inverse ETFs, or gold, investors can also reduce their exposure to market opportunities and other benefits that may arise from their dividend stocks. Therefore, investors need to hedge only a portion of their portfolio that matches their risk tolerance and investment objectives and not over-hedge their portfolio, which may compromise their returns and increase their costs. A general rule of thumb is to hedge no more than 20% to 30% of the portfolio value, depending on the level of risk and uncertainty in the market. Investors also need to monitor and adjust their hedging strategies periodically, as market conditions and dividend stock performance may change over time.

Diversification as a Risk Management Tool

Diversification is a risk management tool that involves spreading your investments across different assets, sectors, industries, or companies that have a low or negative correlation with each other. Diversification can help reduce the overall risk and volatility of your portfolio, as it can lower the impact of any single or group of assets that may underperform or lose value due to various factors.

Diversification is especially important for dividend stock investors, as it can reduce their exposure to specific sectors, industries, or companies that may underperform or cut dividends. Dividend stocks are shares of companies that pay out a portion of their earnings to shareholders regularly, usually quarterly or annually. Dividend stocks can offer investors several benefits, such as stable cash flow, capital appreciation, tax advantages, and protection against inflation. However, dividend stocks are not risk-free, and investors need to be aware of the potential pitfalls and challenges that may arise in this type of investment.

Some of the risks that dividend stock investors may face include:

1. **Sector Risk:** This is the risk of investing in a specific sector of the economy, such as energy, utilities, or financials, that may be affected by cyclical or structural factors, such as demand and supply, regulation, competition, innovation, etc. For example, energy stocks may suffer during periods of low oil prices or environmental concerns, while financial stocks may suffer during periods of low-interest rates or credit crises.

2. **Industry Risk:** This is the risk of investing in a specific industry within a sector, such as airlines, hotels, or banks, that may be affected by industry-specific factors, such as consumer preferences, technological changes, operational issues, etc. For example, airline stocks may suffer during periods of travel restrictions or health emergencies, while hotel stocks may suffer during periods of low occupancy or high competition.

3. **Company Risk:** This is the risk of investing in a specific company within an industry or sector that may be affected by company-specific factors, such as earnings, cash flow, debt, dividends, management, strategy, etc. For example, a company may underperform its peers or the market due to poor financial results or performance, or it may cut or suspend its dividends due to financial distress or operational challenges.

To diversify their portfolio across different dimensions and reduce these risks, dividend stock investors can diversify their portfolio across different dimensions, such as geography, market capitalization, dividend yield, dividend growth, payout ratio, and business model. Here are some guidelines on how to diversify their portfolio across these dimensions:

Geography

This is the dimension of diversifying your portfolio across different countries or regions of the world, such as North America, Europe, Asia, etc. Geography can help you reduce the risk of investing in a single market that may be affected by local or regional factors, such as political instability, currency fluctuations, trade wars, etc. For example, if you invest in dividend stocks from different countries or regions, you can benefit from the growth and stability of different economies and markets and hedge against the decline or volatility of any single market. You can also benefit from the diversification of currency exposure and tax treatment of dividends across different countries or regions. To diversify your portfolio by geography, you can invest in dividend stocks from different countries or regions directly, or you can invest in international or global dividend ETFs or mutual funds that track the performance of dividend stocks from different countries or regions.

Market Capitalization

This is the dimension of diversifying your portfolio across different sizes of companies, measured by their total market value or the number of shares outstanding multiplied by the share price. Market capitalization can help you reduce the risk of investing in a single-size category of companies that may have different characteristics and performance. For example, large-cap companies are generally more established, stable, and profitable than small-cap companies, but they may also have lower growth potential and lower dividend yields. Small-cap companies are generally more innovative, dynamic, and agile than large-cap companies, but they may also have higher volatility and lower dividend safety. To diversify your portfolio by market capitalization, you can invest in dividend stocks from different size categories directly, or you can invest in small-cap, mid-cap, or large-cap dividend ETFs or mutual funds that track the performance of dividend stocks from different size categories.

Dividend Yield

This is the dimension of diversifying your portfolio across different levels of dividend payments relative to the share price, expressed as a percentage. Dividend yield can help you reduce the risk of investing in a single level of dividend income that may not match your income needs and expectations. For example, high-yield dividend stocks are dividend stocks that pay high dividends relative to their share price, usually above 4%. High-yield dividend stocks can offer higher income and higher returns than low-yield dividend stocks, but they may also have lower growth potential and lower dividend safety. Low-yield dividend stocks are dividend stocks that pay low dividends relative to their share price, usually below 2%. Low-yield dividend stocks can offer lower income and lower returns than high-yield dividend stocks, but they may also have higher growth potential and higher dividend safety. To diversify your portfolio by dividend yield, you can invest in dividend stocks with different dividend yields directly, or you can invest in high-yield, low-yield, or blended dividend ETFs or mutual funds that track the performance of dividend stocks with different dividend yields.

Dividend Growth

This is the dimension of diversifying your portfolio across different rates of dividend increases over time, expressed as a percentage. Dividend growth can help you reduce the risk of investing in a single rate of dividend income growth that may not match your income growth and inflation expectations. For example, dividend growth stocks are dividend stocks that have consistently increased their dividends over a long period, usually at least 10 years. Dividend growth stocks can offer higher income growth and higher returns than dividend-cut or stagnant stocks, but they may also have lower dividend yields and lower dividend safety. Dividend cut or stagnant stocks are dividend stocks that have reduced or maintained their dividends over a long period, usually at least 10 years. Dividend cuts or stagnant stocks can offer lower income growth and lower returns than dividend-growth stocks, but they may also have higher dividend yields and higher dividend safety. To diversify your portfolio by dividend growth, you can invest in dividend stocks with different dividend growth rates directly, or you can invest in dividend growth, dividend cut, or dividend stagnant ETFs or mutual funds that track the performance of dividend stocks with different dividend growth rates.

Payout Ratio

This is the dimension of diversifying your portfolio across different proportions of earnings paid out as dividends, expressed as a percentage. The payout ratio can help you reduce the risk of investing in a single proportion of earnings distribution that may not match your income sustainability and reinvestment expectations. For example, high-payout ratio stocks are dividend stocks that pay out a high proportion of their earnings as dividends, usually above 80%. High-payout ratio stocks can offer higher income and higher returns than low-payout ratio stocks, but they may also have lower growth potential and lower dividend safety. Low-payout ratio stocks are dividend stocks that pay out a low proportion of their earnings as dividends, usually below 40%. Low-payout ratio stocks can offer lower income and lower returns than high-payout ratio stocks, but they may also have higher growth potential and higher dividend safety. To diversify your portfolio by payout ratio, you can invest in dividend stocks with different payout ratios directly, or you can invest in high-payout ratio, low-payout ratio, or blended payout ratio ETFs or mutual funds that track the performance of dividend stocks with different payout ratios.

Business Model

This is the dimension of diversifying your portfolio across different types of businesses that generate and distribute their earnings and dividends, such as real estate investment trusts (REITs), master limited partnerships (MLPs), business development companies (BDCs), etc Business model can help you reduce the risk of investing in a single type of business that may have different characteristics and performance. For example, REITs are companies that own and operate real estate properties and payout at least 90% of their taxable income as dividends to shareholders. REITs can offer higher income and higher returns than non-REITs, but they may also have higher volatility and lower tax efficiency. MLPs are partnerships that own and operate energy-related assets and pay out most of their cash flow as distributions to shareholders. MLPs can offer higher income and higher returns than non-MLPs, but they may also have higher complexity and lower liquidity. BDCs are companies that provide financing and advisory services to small and medium-sized businesses and payout at least 90% of their taxable income as dividends to shareholders. BDCs can offer higher income and higher returns than non-BDCs, but they may also have higher risk and lower transparency. To diversify your portfolio by business model, you can invest in dividend stocks with different business models directly, or you can invest in REIT, MLP, BDC, or other business model ETFs or mutual funds that track the performance of dividend stocks with different business models.

Some diversified dividend ETFs or mutual funds that can help you achieve your diversification goals are:

1. **Vanguard High Dividend Yield ETF (VYM):** This is an ETF that tracks the performance of the FTSE High Dividend Yield Index, which consists of large-cap US companies that pay above-average dividends. This ETF can help you diversify your portfolio by market capitalization and dividend yield, as it invests in large-cap dividend stocks with high dividend yields. The ETF has an expense ratio of 0.06% and a dividend yield of 3.01% as of September 1, 2023.

2. **SPDR S&P Dividend ETF (SDY):** This is an ETF that tracks the performance of the S&P High Yield Dividend Aristocrats Index, which consists of US companies that have increased their

dividends for at least 20 consecutive years. This ETF can help you diversify your portfolio by dividend growth and payout ratio, as it invests in dividend growth stocks with moderate payout ratios. The ETF has an expense ratio of 0.35% and a dividend yield of 2.54% as of September 1, 2023.

3. **iShares International Select Dividend ETF (IDV):** This is an ETF that tracks the performance of the Dow Jones EPAC Select Dividend Index, which consists of companies from developed markets outside the US that pay high dividends. This ETF can help you diversify your portfolio by geography and dividend yield, as it invests in international dividend stocks with high dividend yields. The ETF has an expense ratio of 0.49% and a dividend yield of 4.67% as of September 1, 2023.

4. **Schwab US Dividend Equity ETF (SCHD):** This is an ETF that tracks the performance of the Dow Jones U.S. Dividend 100 Index, which consists of US companies that have paid dividends for at least 10 consecutive years and meet certain criteria for quality and value. This ETF can help you diversify your portfolio by market capitalization, dividend yield, dividend growth, and payout ratio, as it invests in large-cap dividend stocks with moderate dividend yields, high dividend growth rates, and low payout ratios. The ETF has an expense ratio of 0.06% and a dividend yield of 2.87% as of September 1, 2023.

5. **Vanguard Real Estate Index Fund Admiral Shares (VGSLX):** This is a mutual fund that tracks the performance of the MSCI US Investable Market Real Estate 25/50 Index, which consists of US companies that own and operate real estate properties or provide real estate services. This fund can help you diversify your portfolio by business model and sector, as it invests in REITs and other real estate-related companies. The fund has an expense ratio of 0.12% and a dividend yield of 2.95% as of August 31, 2023.

Company-Specific News and Dividend Stocks

Company-specific news can have a significant impact on dividend payments, as they can reflect the financial health and performance of dividend-paying companies. Dividend payments are distributions of a portion of a company's earnings to its shareholders, usually on a regular basis. Dividend payments can offer investors several benefits, such as stable income, capital appreciation, tax advantages, and protection against inflation. However, dividend payments are not guaranteed, and companies can change their dividend policies depending on various factors, such as earnings, cash flow, debt, growth, regulation, etc.

Some examples of company-specific news that may affect dividend payments are:

Earnings Reports

Earnings reports are financial statements that show the revenues, expenses, and profits or losses of a company for a specific time, usually quarterly or annually. Earnings reports can affect dividend payments, as they indicate the profitability and sustainability of a company's business operations.

For example, if a company reports higher-than-expected earnings or beats analysts' estimates, it may increase its dividend payments to reward its shareholders and signal its confidence in its future prospects. Conversely, if a company reports lower-than-expected earnings or misses analysts' estimates, it may reduce or suspend its dividend payments to conserve cash and cope with its challenges.

Dividend Announcements

Dividend announcements are official statements that declare the amount, date, and frequency of dividend payments by a company to its shareholders. Dividend announcements can affect dividend payments, as they reveal the current and future dividend policies of a company. For example, if a company announces an increase in its dividend amount or frequency, it may boost its share price and attract more investors who seek higher income and returns. Conversely, if a company announces a decrease or suspension in its dividend amount or frequency, it may lower its share price and deter investors who seek stable income and returns.

Mergers and Acquisitions

Mergers and acquisitions are transactions that involve the combination or takeover of two or more companies into one entity. Mergers and acquisitions can affect dividend payments, as they can change the financial structure and performance of the combined entity. For example, if a company merges with or acquires another company that has higher earnings or growth potential than itself, it may increase its dividend payments to reflect its improved financial position and outlook. Conversely, if a company merges with or acquires another company that has lower earnings or growth potential than itself, it may reduce or suspend its dividend payments to cover the costs and risks of the transaction.

Lawsuits

Lawsuits are legal actions that involve disputes or claims between two or more parties in a court of law. Lawsuits can affect dividend payments, as they can result in financial losses or damages for a company that is sued or sued by another party. For example, if a company is sued by a customer, competitor, regulator, or other party for breach of contract, patent infringement, antitrust violation, or other legal issues, it may incur financial losses or damages that may reduce its earnings or cash flow, and thus affect its ability to pay dividends. Conversely, if a company sues another party for compensation, restitution, or other legal remedies, it may receive financial gains or benefits that may increase its earnings or cash flow and thus enhance its ability to pay dividends.

Scandals

Scandals are events that involve wrongdoing, misconduct, or controversy by a company or its employees, managers, or directors. Scandals can affect dividend payments, as they can damage the reputation and credibility of a company and its products or services. For example, if a company is involved in a scandal such as fraud, corruption, bribery, data breach, environmental harm, or human rights violation, it may face public backlash, customer boycotts, regulatory investigations, or legal actions that may harm its sales, profits, or market value, and thus affect its ability to pay dividends.

To interpret and respond to company-specific news that may affect dividend payments, dividend stock investors can use fundamental analysis and technical analysis to evaluate the financial health and performance of dividend-paying companies.

Fundamental Analysis

Fundamental analysis is a method of evaluating the intrinsic value and quality of a company based on its financial statements, ratios, indicators, and metrics. Fundamental analysis can help investors assess the profitability, growth, stability, efficiency, and sustainability of a company's business operations and dividend payments. Some examples of fundamental analysis tools and techniques are:

- Earnings per share (EPS)
- Dividend per share (DPS)
- Dividend payout ratio
- Dividend yield

To interpret and respond to company-specific news that may affect dividend payments, investors need to use fundamental analysis tools and techniques to evaluate the financial health and performance of dividend-paying companies. They also need to compare the company's results and guidance with analysts' estimates and expectations and monitor the market reaction and sentiment. Depending on their findings and conclusions, investors may decide to buy, hold, or sell their dividend stocks or adjust their portfolio allocation accordingly.

Technical Analysis

Technical analysis is a method of evaluating the price movements and trends of a company based on its historical trading data, such as price, volume, momentum, etc. Technical analysis can help investors identify the patterns and signals that indicate the direction and strength of a company's share price and dividend payments. Some examples of technical analysis tools and techniques are:

1. **Moving Averages:** Moving averages are lines that show the average price of a company's share over a certain time, such as 50 days, 100 days, or 200 days. Moving averages can indicate the trend and momentum of a company's share price and dividend payments. A rising moving average means that the share price is increasing, and the dividend payments are likely to be stable or growing. A falling moving average means that the share price is decreasing, and the dividend payments are likely to be unstable or declining. A crossover between two moving averages of different periods can indicate a change in trend or momentum. For example, if the 50-day moving average crosses above the 200-day moving average, it is called a golden cross, which signals a bullish trend or momentum. Conversely, if the 50-day moving average crosses below the 200-day moving average, it is called a death cross, which signals a bearish trend or momentum.

2. **Support and Resistance:** Support and resistance are levels that show the minimum and maximum price that a company's share tends to reach before reversing its direction. Support is the level that prevents the share price from falling further, while resistance is the level that prevents the share price from rising further. Support and resistance can indicate the range and volatility of a company's share price and dividend payments. A break above resistance or below support can indicate a breakout or breakdown of the share price and dividend payments. For example, if the share price breaks above resistance, it may signal an upward trend or momentum and higher dividend payments. Conversely, if the share price breaks below support, it may signal a downward trend or momentum and lower dividend payments.

3. **Indicators and Oscillators:** Indicators and oscillators are mathematical calculations that show the various aspects of a company's share price movement, such as trend, momentum, strength, volatility, etc. Indicators and oscillators can indicate the current and future direction and magnitude of a company's share price and dividend payments. Some examples of indicators and oscillators are relative strength index (RSI), moving average convergence divergence (MACD), stochastic oscillator, etc. For example, RSI measures the speed and change of price movements on a scale from 0 to 100. A high RSI (above 70) means that the share price is overbought and may reverse its direction soon. A low RSI (below 30) means that the share price is oversold and may reverse its direction soon. MACD measures the difference between two moving averages of different periods. A positive MACD means that the share price is in an upward trend and may increase further. A negative MACD means that the share price is in a downward trend and may decrease further. The stochastic oscillator measures the position of the share price relative to its high-low range over a certain period. A high stochastic (above 80) means that the share price is near its high and may reverse its direction soon. A low stochastic (below 20) means that the share price is near its low and may reverse its direction soon.

Some sources of reliable and timely information on dividend stocks are:

1. **Financial Websites:** Financial websites are online platforms that provide various types of information on dividend stocks, such as prices, charts, news, analysis, ratings, dividends, etc. Some examples of financial websites are Yahoo Finance, MarketBeat, Seeking Alpha, etc.

2. **Newsletters:** Newsletters are publications that provide regular updates and insights on dividend stocks, such as recommendations, strategies, tips, trends, etc. Some examples of newsletters are The Motley Fool Income Investor, Dividend Investor, Dividend Detective, etc.

3. **Podcasts:** Podcasts are audio or video programs that provide discussions and interviews on dividend stocks, such as opinions, experiences, stories, advice, etc. Some examples of podcasts are The Dividend Guy Podcast, The Dividend Cafe, The Canadian Dividend Growth Podcast, etc.

4. **Blogs:** Blogs are websites that provide personal or professional opinions and perspectives on dividend stocks, such as reviews, comparisons, case studies, portfolios, etc. Some examples of blogs are Sure Dividend, Dividend Growth Investor, Dividend Diplomats, etc.

Chapter 7

Taxation and Legal Considerations

Dividend stock trading can provide investors with a steady stream of income, as well as the potential for capital appreciation.

However, dividend stock trading also comes with its own set of tax and legal implications that investors need to understand and follow. Taxes and legal regulations can affect the profitability and viability of dividend stock trading, as well as the rights and responsibilities of investors. Ignoring or violating these rules and requirements can result in penalties, fines, or even criminal charges.

Therefore, dividend stock traders need to be aware of the tax and legal aspects of their investment strategy and to plan accordingly. This chapter will help you navigate the tax and legal landscape of dividend stock trading and provide you with some tips and best practices to optimize your trading performance.

Tax Implications of Dividend Income and Capital Gains

Dividend income and capital gains are two types of income that investors can earn from dividend stock trading. Dividend income is the payment that a company makes to its shareholders, usually from its earnings or profits. Capital gains are the profits that an investor makes when selling a stock at a higher price than the purchase price. Both dividend income and capital gains are subject to taxation, but they are taxed differently depending on various factors. This essay will explain how dividend income and capital gains are taxed, compare the tax rates for different types of dividends and capital gains, discuss the factors that affect the tax treatment of dividends and capital gains, provide examples and calculations to illustrate the tax impact of different dividend and capital gain scenarios, and suggest some strategies to minimize taxes on dividends and capital gains.

How Dividend Income and Capital Gains Are Taxed

Dividend income and capital gains are taxed differently because they are classified as different types of income by the Internal Revenue Service (IRS). Dividend income is considered ordinary income, which means it is added to the investor's other sources of income, such as wages, salaries, interest, and rents, and taxed at the investor's marginal tax rate. The marginal tax rate is the tax rate that applies to the last dollar of taxable income. For example, if an investor's taxable income is $50,000 and their marginal tax rate is 22%, they will pay 22% tax on their dividend income.

Capital gains, on the other hand, are considered investment income, which means they are taxed separately from the investor's ordinary income at a preferential tax rate. The preferential tax rate is lower than the marginal tax rate, and it depends on how long the investor holds the stock before selling it. If the investor holds the stock for more than one year, they will have a long-term capital gain, which is taxed at 0%, 15%, or 20%, depending on their income level. If the investor holds the stock for one year or less, they will have a short-term capital gain, which is taxed at their marginal tax rate.

Tax Rates for Different Types of Dividends and Capital Gains

Not all dividends and capital gains are taxed equally. There are different types of dividends and capital gains that have different tax rates. The main types of dividends are qualified dividends and non-qualified dividends. Qualified dividends are dividends that meet certain requirements set by the IRS, such as being paid by a U.S. corporation or a foreign corporation that is eligible for certain tax treaties and being held by the investor for more than 60 days during 121 days around the ex-dividend date. Non-qualified dividends are dividends that do not meet these requirements, such as dividends paid by real estate investment trusts (REITs), master limited partnerships (MLPs), or certain foreign corporations.

Qualified dividends are taxed at the same preferential tax rate as long-term capital gains, which are 0%, 15%, or 20%, depending on the investor's income level. Non-qualified dividends are taxed at the same marginal tax rate as ordinary income, which can range from 10% to 37%, depending on the investor's income level.

The main types of capital gains are short-term capital gains and long-term capital gains. Short-term capital gains are profits from selling stocks that were held for one year or less. Long-term capital gains are profits from selling stocks that were held for more than one year. Short-term capital gains are taxed at the same marginal tax rate as ordinary income, which can range from 10% to 37%, depending on the investor's income level. Long-term capital gains are taxed at a preferential tax rate of 0%, 15%, or 20%, depending on the investor's income level.

Factors That Affect the Tax Treatment of Dividends and Capital Gains

The tax treatment of dividends and capital gains depends on several factors, such as the holding period, the income level, and the filing status of the investor. The holding period is the length of time that an investor owns a stock before selling it. The holding period determines whether a dividend is qualified or non-qualified and whether a capital gain is short-term or long-term. The longer the holding period, the more likely it is that a dividend will be qualified and a capital gain will be long-term, which means lower taxes.

The income level is the amount of taxable income that an investor has in a given year. The income level determines the marginal tax rate for ordinary income and non-qualified dividends and the preferential tax rate for qualified dividends and long-term capital gains. The higher the income level, the higher the tax rate for both types of income.

The filing status is the category that an investor chooses when filing their tax return, such as single, married filing jointly, married filing separately, or head of household. The filing status affects the income thresholds that determine the tax rates for qualified dividends and long-term capital gains. For example, in 2021, a single filer will pay 0% tax on qualified dividends and long-term capital gains if their taxable income is less than $40,400, 15% tax if their taxable income is between $40,400 and $445,850, and 20% tax if their taxable income is more than $445,850. However, a married couple filing jointly will pay 0% tax on qualified dividends and long-term capital gains if their taxable income is less than $80,800, 15% tax if their taxable income is between $80,800 and $501,600, and 20% tax if their taxable income is more than $501,600.

Strategies to Minimize Taxes on Dividends and Capital Gains

There are some strategies that investors can use to minimize taxes on dividends and capital gains from dividend stock trading. Some of these strategies are:

1. **Tax-Loss Harvesting:** This is a strategy that involves selling stocks that have declined in value to offset the gains from other stocks. This can reduce the taxable income and lower the tax liability. However, investors need to be careful of the wash sale rule, which prevents them from claiming a loss if they buy back the same or substantially identical stock within 30 days before or after the sale.

2. **Asset Allocation:** This is a strategy that involves diversifying the portfolio across different types of assets, such as stocks, bonds, cash, and real estate. This can reduce the overall risk and volatility of the portfolio, as well as optimize tax efficiency. For example, investors can allocate more of their assets to tax-advantaged accounts, such as IRAs or 401(k) plans, where they can defer or avoid taxes on dividends and capital gains. They can also allocate more of their assets to qualified dividends and long-term capital gains, which have lower tax rates than non-qualified dividends and short-term capital gains.

3. **Dividend Reinvestment:** This is a strategy that involves using the dividends received from stocks to buy more shares of the same stocks. This can increase the compounding effect and growth potential of the portfolio, as well as defer taxes on dividends until the stocks are sold. However, investors need to keep track of their cost basis and dividend reinvestment history, as they will still owe taxes on the dividends when they sell the stocks.

Tax-Advantaged Accounts for Dividend Stock Trading

Tax-advantaged accounts are special types of accounts that offer tax benefits for investors who use them for saving and investing purposes. Tax-advantaged accounts can help dividend stock traders save taxes on their dividend income and capital gains, as well as enhance their trading strategy's effectiveness. There are different types of tax-advantaged accounts, such as individual retirement accounts (IRAs), 401(k) plans, health savings accounts (HSAs), and 529 plans. Each type of account has its own features, advantages, and disadvantages, such as contribution limits, withdrawal rules, investment options, and fees. This essay will describe the main types of tax-advantaged accounts, compare the pros and cons of each type of account, provide examples and calculations to show the potential tax savings from using tax-advantaged accounts for dividend stock trading, and recommend some best practices for choosing and managing tax-advantaged accounts.

Types of Tax-Advantaged Accounts

The main types of tax-advantaged accounts that dividend stock traders can use are:

1. **Individual Retirement Accounts (IRAs):** These are personal savings accounts that allow investors to save for retirement. There are two types of IRAs: traditional IRAs and Roth IRAs. Traditional IRAs allow investors to make pre-tax contributions, which means they can deduct their contributions from their taxable income in the year they make them. However, they have to pay taxes on their withdrawals in retirement at their ordinary income tax rate. Roth IRAs allow investors to make after-tax contributions, which means they cannot deduct their contributions from their taxable income in the year they make them. However, they can withdraw their money tax-free in retirement as long as they meet certain requirements. Both types of IRAs have a contribution limit of $6,000 per year ($7,000 if age 50 or older) in 2021. Investors can invest in a variety of assets within their IRAs, including dividend stocks.

2. **401(k) Plans:** These are employer-sponsored retirement plans that allow employees to save for retirement through payroll deductions. There are two types of 401(k) plans: traditional 401(k) plans and Roth 401(k) plans. Traditional 401(k) plans allow employees to make pre-tax contributions, which means they can reduce their taxable income in the year they make them. However, they have to pay taxes on their withdrawals in retirement at their ordinary income tax rate. Roth 401(k) plans allow employees to make after-tax contributions, which means they cannot reduce their taxable income in the year they make them. However, they can withdraw their money tax-free in retirement as long as they meet certain requirements. Both types of 401(k) plans have a contribution limit of $19,500 per year ($26,000 if age 50 or older) in 2021. Employers may also match a portion of the employee's contributions, which is an additional benefit. Employees can invest in a variety of assets within their 401(k) plans, including dividend stocks.

3. **Health Savings Accounts (HSAs):** These are savings accounts that allow individuals with high-deductible health plans (HDHPs) to save for medical expenses. HSAs allow individuals to make pre-tax contributions, which means they can deduct their contributions from their taxable income in the year they make them. They can also withdraw their money tax-free for qualified medical expenses at any time. Additionally, they can invest their money in a

variety of assets within their HSAs, including dividend stocks. HSAs have a contribution limit of $3,600 for individuals and $7,200 for families in 2021.

4. **529 Plans:** These are savings plans that allow individuals to save for education expenses. There are two types of 529 plans: prepaid tuition plans and education savings plans. Prepaid tuition plans allow individuals to pay for future tuition at current prices at participating colleges and universities. Education savings plans allow individuals to invest in a variety of assets within their 529 plans, including dividend stocks. They can withdraw their money tax-free for qualified education expenses at any time. 529 plans do not have a federal contribution limit, but each state may have its own limit.

Pros and Cons of Each Type of Account

Each type of tax-advantaged account has its own pros and cons for dividend stock traders. Some of the pros and cons are:

1. **IRAs:** The pros of IRAs are that they offer flexibility and control over investment choices, they allow investors to defer or avoid taxes on dividends and capital gains within the account, and they provide an opportunity to save for retirement. The cons of IRAs are that they have relatively low contribution limits compared to other types of accounts, they have early withdrawal penalties if investors take out money before age 59½ (unless they qualify for an exception), and they may have income limits or phase-outs that restrict the eligibility or deductibility of contributions for some investors.

2. **401(k) Plans:** The pros of 401(k) plans are that they offer higher contribution limits than IRAs, they allow investors to defer or avoid taxes on dividends and capital gains within the account, they provide an opportunity to save for retirement, and they may have employer matching contributions that increase the savings potential. The cons of 401(k) plans are that they have less flexibility and control over the investment choices, they have early withdrawal penalties if employees take out money before age 59½ (unless they qualify for an exception), and they may have fees or expenses that reduce the returns.

3. **HSAs:** The pros of HSAs are that they offer triple tax benefits: pre-tax contributions, tax-free withdrawals for qualified medical expenses, and tax-deferred or tax-free growth within the account. They also allow investors to invest in dividend stocks and other assets within the account, and they do not have a time limit for using the funds. The cons of HSAs are that they require individuals to have an HDHP, which may have higher deductibles and out-of-pocket costs than other types of health plans, they have relatively low contribution limits compared to other types of accounts, and they have penalties for non-qualified withdrawals.

4. **529 Plans:** The pros of 529 plans are that they allow investors to save for education expenses for themselves or their beneficiaries, they allow investors to invest in dividend stocks and other assets within the account, and they provide tax-free withdrawals for

qualified education expenses. The cons of 529 plans are that they have penalties for non-qualified withdrawals, they may have fees or expenses that reduce the returns, and they may affect the eligibility for financial aid or scholarships.

Legal Considerations and Compliance Requirements for Dividend Stock Trading

Here are some of the main aspects to consider:

1. **Taxation:** Dividends are generally taxable as ordinary income unless they qualify as qualified dividends, which are taxed at a lower rate. Qualified dividends are paid by U.S. corporations or foreign corporations that meet certain criteria, such as being traded on a U.S. exchange or having a tax treaty with the U.S. To qualify for the lower tax rate, the trader must also meet the holding period requirement, which means holding the stock for more than 60 days during the 121-day period that begins 60 days before the ex-dividend date. The ex-dividend date is the date when the stock trades without the right to receive the dividend. Traders should also be aware of the wash sale rule, which disallows the deduction of losses from selling a stock if the trader buys a substantially identical stock within 30 days before or after the sale.

2. **Regulation:** Dividend stock trading is subject to the same securities laws and regulations as any other type of stock trading. Traders must comply with the rules and regulations of the Securities and Exchange Commission (SEC), the Financial Industry Regulatory Authority (FINRA), and any other relevant authorities. Some of the key rules and regulations include:

   - The Securities Act of 1933 requires companies to register their securities offerings with the SEC and provide investors with adequate disclosure of material information.

   - The Securities Exchange Act of 1934 regulates the secondary market for securities, including trading activities, reporting requirements, and anti-fraud provisions.

   - The Investment Company Act of 1940 regulates mutual funds and other types of investment companies that invest in dividend stocks.

   - The Investment Advisers Act of 1940 regulates individuals and firms that provide investment advice or manage portfolios of dividend stocks for a fee.

   - FINRA rules, which govern the conduct and supervision of brokers and dealers that facilitate dividend stock trading.

3. **Risks:** Dividend stock trading involves various risks that traders should be prepared for. Some of the common risks include:

- **Market Risk**: The risk that the price of a dividend stock will fluctuate due to changes in market conditions, such as supply and demand, economic factors, political events, or investor sentiment.

- **Dividend Risk**: The risk that a company will reduce or eliminate its dividend payments due to financial difficulties, strategic decisions, or regulatory constraints.

- **Liquidity Risk**: The risk that a trader will not be able to buy or sell a dividend stock quickly or at a favorable price due to low trading volume or market disruptions.

- **Credit Risk:** The risk that a company will default on its debt obligations, which could impair its ability to pay dividends or affect its credit rating.

Dividend stock trading can be a rewarding strategy for investors who seek income and growth, but it also requires careful planning and execution.

Chapter 8

The Psychological Aspect of Dividend Stock Trading

Trading psychology is a critical component of successful dividend stock trading. It is the study of how emotions, cognition, and personality affect trading behavior and outcomes. Trading psychology can help traders understand their own strengths and weaknesses, as well as the opportunities and threats in the market.

Dividend stock trading involves investing in companies that pay regular dividends to their shareholders. Dividends are a portion of the company's profits that are distributed to the owners of the stock. Dividend stock trading can provide a steady source of income and capital appreciation for investors.

However, dividend stock trading also involves uncertainties and risks. The market can be volatile and unpredictable, and dividend payments can be reduced or suspended by the company. Traders may face emotional biases and impulsive decision-making tendencies that can hinder their trading success. For example, traders may become overconfident, loss-averse, confirmation-biased, or recency-biased.

Therefore, it is important to develop a healthy trading mindset that can cope with the uncertainties and risks of the market. A healthy trading mindset is rational, objective, disciplined, and resilient. It can help traders avoid emotional reactions and impulse trades and instead follow a sound trading strategy based on analysis and evidence.

Common Psychological Pitfalls

One of the biggest challenges for dividend stock traders is to overcome their own emotional biases and impulsive decision-making tendencies. These psychological pitfalls can interfere with the trader's ability to analyze the market objectively, follow a sound trading strategy, and execute trades effectively.

Overconfidence: Overconfidence is the tendency to overestimate one's own abilities and knowledge, leading to excessive risk-taking and ignoring relevant information. Overconfident traders may believe that they have superior skills or insights that can beat the market and disregard the role of luck or randomness in trading outcomes. They may also ignore or downplay the risks involved in their trades and fail to diversify their portfolio or use proper risk management techniques. Overconfidence can lead to taking on too much leverage, entering or exiting trades at the wrong time, or holding on to losing positions too long in the hope of a reversal.

Loss Aversion: Loss aversion is the tendency to prefer avoiding losses over acquiring gains, leading to holding on to losing positions too long or selling winning positions too soon. Loss-averse traders may experience a stronger emotional impact from losing money than from making money and thus try to avoid realizing losses at all costs. They may also exhibit a disposition effect, which is the tendency to sell stocks that have risen in value and keep stocks that have fallen in value, contrary to the buy-low-sell-high principle. Loss aversion can lead to missing out on profitable opportunities, locking in small profits while letting losses grow, or averaging down on losing positions without a valid reason.

Confirmation Bias: Confirmation bias is the tendency to seek out, interpret, and remember information that confirms one's existing beliefs, leading to ignoring or dismissing contrary evidence. Confirmation-biased traders may have a preconceived notion about the direction or value of a stock or the market and only pay attention to information that supports their view. They may also filter out or rationalize information that challenges their view or attribute their successes to their own skills and their failures to external factors. Confirmation bias can lead to being overconfident in one's predictions, failing to update one's beliefs based on new data, or sticking to a faulty trading strategy despite poor results.

Recency Bias: Recency bias is the tendency to give more weight to recent events than to long-term trends, leading to chasing performance or abandoning a sound strategy. Recency-biased traders may be influenced by the latest news, market movements, or trading outcomes, and extrapolate them into the future. They may also forget or neglect the historical patterns, averages, or cycles of the market or a stock. Recency bias can lead to being overly optimistic or pessimistic about the market or a stock, following the herd mentality, jumping on bandwagons, or switching strategies too frequently based on short-term results.

Strategies for Overcoming Psychological Challenges

Trading psychology is not only about avoiding common psychological pitfalls but also about developing positive psychological skills and habits that can enhance one's trading performance. In this section, you will learn some practical strategies for overcoming the psychological challenges that dividend stock traders may face and fostering a healthy trading mindset. These strategies are:

Practicing Mindfulness

Mindfulness is the practice of paying attention to the present moment with openness and curiosity, without judgment or attachment. Mindfulness can help traders reduce stress, increase awareness, and improve decision-making. By practicing mindfulness, traders can become more aware of their own emotions, thoughts, and sensations and how they affect their trading behavior. They can also become more attentive to market signals, trends, and opportunities and avoid being distracted by irrelevant or misleading information. Mindfulness can also help traders cope with uncertainty and volatility and accept the outcomes of their trades without regret or resentment. Some ways to practice mindfulness are:

1. **Meditating Regularly**: Meditation is a technique that involves focusing one's attention on a chosen object, such as one's breath, a word, or a sound, and observing one's thoughts and feelings without reacting to them. Meditation can help traders calm their minds, relax their bodies, and enhance their concentration and clarity. There are many types of meditation, such as breathing meditation, mantra meditation, or guided meditation, that traders can choose from according to their preference and convenience.

2. **Keeping a Trading Journal**: A trading journal is a record of one's trading activities, results, and reflections. A trading journal can help traders track their performance, identify their strengths and weaknesses, and learn from their mistakes and successes. A trading journal can also help traders monitor their emotional state, recognize their psychological biases, and evaluate their trading decisions. By keeping a trading journal, traders can become more mindful of their trading process and outcomes and improve their trading skills and strategies.

3. **Practicing Gratitude**: Gratitude is the feeling of appreciation for what one has or receives. Gratitude can help traders cultivate a positive attitude towards trading and life in general. By practicing gratitude, traders can acknowledge the benefits and opportunities that trading provides them, such as income, growth, challenge, and enjoyment. They can also appreciate the factors that contribute to their trading success, such as their own efforts, skills, knowledge, and resources. Gratitude can also help traders cope with losses and setbacks by reminding them of the bigger picture and the long-term goals.

Maintaining Discipline During Market Fluctuations

Discipline is the practice of sticking to a predefined trading plan and following consistent rules and criteria for entering and exiting trades, regardless of market conditions. Discipline can help traders avoid emotional reactions and impulse trades that can result from market fluctuations. By maintaining discipline, traders can trade with confidence, consistency, and rationality. Some ways to maintain discipline are:

1. **Developing a Clear Trading Plan**: A trading plan is a document that outlines one's trading goals, strategies, methods, rules, and criteria. A trading plan can help traders define their trading style, identify their risk-reward ratio, select their entry and exit points, set their stop-losses and take-profits, determine their position size, allocate their capital, measure their performance, and review their results. A trading plan can also help traders avoid

making decisions based on emotions or impulses by providing them with a clear roadmap for each trade.

2. **Following One's Trading Plan Faithfully:** Once a trader has developed a clear trading plan, they should follow it faithfully, without deviating from it or changing it frequently. Following one's trading plan means executing trades according to predefined rules and criteria without being influenced by fear or greed, hope or regret, or any other emotion that may arise during trading. Following one's trading plan also means respecting one's stop-losses and take-profits, without moving them or ignoring them, based on the market movements or one's expectations.

3. **Reviewing One's Trading Plan Periodically**: A trader should review their trading plan periodically to ensure that it is still relevant, effective, and aligned with their goals. Reviewing one's trading plan means analyzing one's performance, results, feedback, and learning outcomes based on the data collected from one's trades (such as from one's trading journal). Reviewing one's trading plan also means making adjustments or improvements to one's plan, if necessary, based on the evidence (such as from backtesting or paper trading).

Managing Stress Effectively

Stress is the physical or emotional response to perceived threats or challenges in the environment. Stress can be beneficial or harmful, depending on its intensity, duration, and frequency. Stress can be beneficial when it motivates one to perform better, learn faster, or adapt to change. Stress can be harmful when it overwhelms one's coping resources, impairs one's functioning, or damages one's health. Trading can be a stressful activity, as it involves uncertainties, risks, losses, and pressures. Therefore, traders need to manage their stress effectively to prevent it from affecting their trading performance and well-being. Some ways to manage stress effectively are:

1. **Exercising Regularly:** Exercise is a physical activity that involves moving one's body and muscles. Exercise can help traders reduce stress by releasing endorphins (the natural painkillers and mood boosters of the body), improving blood circulation, enhancing oxygen delivery, and strengthening the immune system. Exercise can also help traders improve their physical fitness, mental alertness, and emotional stability. Some examples of exercise are walking, jogging, cycling, swimming, or playing sports.

2. **Getting Enough Sleep:** Sleep is a state of rest and recovery for the body and mind. Sleep can help traders reduce stress by restoring energy, repairing the tissues, consolidating memory, and regulating the hormones of the body. Sleep can also help traders improve their cognitive functions, such as attention, concentration, learning, and problem-solving. The recommended amount of sleep for adults is 7 to 9 hours per night.

3. **Meditating Regularly:** Meditation is a technique that involves focusing one's attention on a chosen object, such as one's breath, a word, or a sound, and observing one's thoughts and

feelings without reacting to them. Meditation can help traders reduce stress by calming their minds, relaxing their bodies, and enhancing their concentration and clarity. There are many types of meditation, such as breathing meditation, mantra meditation, or guided meditation, that traders can choose from according to their preference and convenience.

4. **Seeking Social Support**: Social support is the assistance or comfort that one receives from others, such as family, friends, colleagues, or mentors. Social support can help traders reduce stress by providing them with emotional, informational, or practical help. Social support can also help traders improve their self-esteem, confidence, and motivation. Some ways to seek social support are:

- Communicating with others who share one's trading interests or goals.

- Joining a trading community or group where one can exchange ideas, feedback, or advice with other traders.

- Seeking guidance or coaching from an experienced or professional trader who can mentor one's trading journey.

Chapter 9

Beyond the Basics: Advanced Dividend Strategies

In this chapter, you will explore some of the more sophisticated techniques that can help you maximize your dividend income and diversify your portfolio. You will learn how to capture dividends from different types of stocks, how to trade around the ex-dividend date, how to use options and derivatives to enhance your dividend strategy, and how to invest in ETFs and mutual funds that focus on dividends. You will also understand the benefits and risks of each technique and how to apply them in different market conditions and scenarios. This chapter will help you take your dividend trading skills to the next level and achieve your financial goals faster and easier. Let's get started!

Dividend Capture Strategies

Dividend capture is a technique that involves buying a stock before its ex-dividend date and selling it shortly after to receive the dividend payment. The goal of dividend capture is to profit from the dividend income without holding the stock for a long time. There are different types of dividend capture strategies, depending on the type and frequency of the dividend, the holding period, and the tax treatment. Some of the common types of dividend capture strategies are:

1. **Regular Dividend Capture**: This is the simplest form of dividend capture, where the investor buys a stock before its ex-dividend date and sells it on or after the ex-dividend date. The investor receives the regular dividend that the company pays quarterly or annually. For example, if a company pays a quarterly dividend of $0.50 per share, and the investor buys 100 shares before the ex-dividend date and sells them on or after the ex-dividend date, the investor will receive $50 in dividend income.

2. **Special Dividend Capture**: This is a variation of regular dividend capture, where the investor targets stocks that pay a special or one-time dividend, which is usually larger than the regular dividend. The investor buys the stock before the ex-dividend date for the special dividend and sells it on or after the ex-dividend date. The investor receives the special dividend in addition to the regular dividend if applicable. For example, if a company pays a special dividend of $5 per share and a regular dividend of $0.50 per share, and the investor buys 100 shares before the ex-dividend date for both dividends and sells them on or after the ex-dividend date, the investor will receive $550 in dividend income.

3. **Preferred Dividend Capture:** This is a type of dividend capture that involves buying and selling preferred stocks, which are hybrid securities that have both equity and debt characteristics. Preferred stocks pay fixed dividends at regular intervals and have priority over common stocks in terms of dividend payments and liquidation. The investor buys the preferred stock before its ex-dividend date and sells it on or after the ex-dividend date. The investor receives the preferred dividend, which is usually higher than the common dividend. For example, if a company pays a preferred dividend of $1 per share quarterly and a common dividend of $0.50 per share quarterly, and the investor buys 100 shares of preferred stock before the ex-dividend date and sells them on, or after the ex-dividend date, the investor will receive $100 in dividend income.

Pros and Cons

Dividend capture strategies have some pros and cons that investors should be aware of before using them. Some of the pros are:

1. **Dividend Income:** Dividend capture strategies can provide a steady stream of income for investors who are looking for cash flow or passive income. Dividends can also help investors reduce their cost basis or increase their return on investment.

2. **Short-Term Holding:** Dividend capture strategies can allow investors to profit from dividends without committing to holding the stock for a long time. This can reduce the exposure to market risk and volatility and free up capital for other opportunities.

3. **Flexibility:** Dividend capture strategies can be applied to different types of stocks, such as common stocks, preferred stocks, REITs, MLPs, etc. Investors can also use different methods to execute their trades, such as limit orders, stop orders, market orders, etc.

Some of the cons are:

1. **Tax Implications:** Dividend capture strategies can have unfavorable tax consequences for investors who are subject to income tax. Dividends are usually taxed at ordinary income rates, which are higher than capital gains rates. Moreover, dividends that are received within 60 days of buying or selling the stock are not qualified for lower tax rates. Therefore, investors should consult their tax advisors before using dividend capture strategies.

2. **Market Volatility:** Dividend capture strategies can expose investors to market fluctuations and price movements that can affect their profitability. The price of the stock can drop by more than the amount of the dividend on or after the ex-dividend date, resulting in a net loss for the investor. The price of the stock can also change due to other factors such as earnings reports, news events, analyst ratings, etc., which can affect the investor's entry and exit points.

3. **Opportunity Cost**: Dividend capture strategies can involve opportunity costs for investors who are sacrificing long-term growth potential for short-term income. By selling the stock shortly after receiving the dividend, investors are missing out on any future appreciation or dividends that the stock may offer. Investors should compare their expected return from dividend capture with their expected return from holding the stock for a longer period.

Ex-Dividend Date Trading

The ex-dividend date is the date on which a stock trades without the right to receive the next dividend payment. This means that anyone who buys the stock on or before the ex-dividend date will not receive the dividend, while anyone who sells the stock on or before the ex-dividend date will receive the dividend. The ex-dividend date is usually one business day before the record date, which is the date on which the company determines who is eligible to receive the dividend.

The ex-dividend date affects the price and value of a stock because it reflects the amount of dividend that is deducted from the stock's value. On the ex-dividend date, the stock price usually drops by approximately the amount of the dividend per share, assuming no other market factors affect the price. For example, if a stock pays a dividend of $0.50 per share, and its price is $50 before the ex-dividend date, its price will likely drop to $49.50 on the ex-dividend date. However, this does not mean that the value of the stock has changed because the investor still owns the same number of shares and will receive the dividend payment later.

There are different ways to trade around the ex-dividend date, depending on the investor's objectives and expectations. Some of the common methods are:

1. **Buying Before and Selling After:** This is a method that involves buying a stock before its ex-dividend date, and selling it on or after the ex-dividend date. The investor receives the dividend payment and hopes that the stock price will recover from the ex-dividend date drop or increase due to other factors. The expected return from this method is equal to the dividend yield plus or minus the capital gain or loss from selling the stock. For example, if an investor buys 100 shares of a stock at $50 before its ex-dividend date, and sells them at $49.80 on or after its ex-dividend date, and receives a dividend of $0.50 per share, the expected return is:

Expected return = (Dividend yield + Capital gain/loss) x 100 Expected return = (($0.50 / $50) + ($49.80 - $50) / $50) x 100 Expected return = (0.01 - 0.004) x 100 Expected return = 0.996%

2. **Selling Before and Buying After**: This is a method that involves selling a stock before its ex-dividend date and buying it back on or after its ex-dividend date. The investor avoids receiving the dividend payment and hopes that the stock price will drop by more than the amount of the dividend on or after its ex-dividend date. The expected return from this method is equal to the capital gain or loss from buying back the stock minus the dividend yield. For example, if an investor sells 100 shares of a stock at $50 before its ex-dividend

date, and buys them back at $49.40 on or after its ex-dividend date, and avoids a dividend of $0.50 per share, the expected return is:

Expected return = (Capital gain/loss - Dividend yield) x 100 Expected return = (($49.40 - $50) / $50 - ($0.50 / $50)) x 100 Expected return = (-0.012 - 0.01) x 100 Expected return = -2.2%

3. **Holding Through:** This is a method that involves holding a stock through its ex-dividend date without buying or selling it. The investor receives the dividend payment and hopes that the stock price will appreciate over time due to other factors. The expected return from this method is equal to the dividend yield plus or minus the capital gain or loss from holding the stock. For example, if an investor holds 100 shares of a stock at $50 before its ex-dividend date, and continues to hold them at $51 on or after its ex-dividend date, and receives a dividend of $0.50 per share, the expected return is:

Expected return = (Dividend yield + Capital gain/loss) x 100 Expected return = (($0.50 / $50) + ($51 - $50) / $50) x 100 Expected return = (0.01 + 0.02) x 100 Expected return = 3%

Factors Influencing Ex-Dividend Date

The factors that influence the ex-dividend date price drop are mainly related to supply and demand forces in the market, as well as investor behavior and expectations. Some of these factors are:

1. **Dividend Yield:** The dividend yield is equal to the annual dividend per share divided by the current stock price. It measures how much income an investor can expect to receive from holding a stock for one year. A higher dividend yield means that a larger portion of the stock's value is attributed to dividends, which can make it more attractive for income-seeking investors. A higher dividend yield can also indicate that a stock is undervalued or has a lower growth potential, which can make it less appealing for growth-oriented investors. Therefore, a higher dividend yield can result in a larger ex-dividend date price drop, as more investors may sell the stock before the ex-dividend date to capture the dividend, and fewer investors may buy the stock on or after the ex-dividend date to avoid the dividend.

2. **Dividend Growth Rate:** The dividend growth rate is equal to the percentage change in the annual dividend per share over time. It measures how much a company increases its dividend payments to shareholders over time. A higher dividend growth rate means that a company is confident and capable of generating more earnings and cash flow, which can make it more attractive for growth-oriented investors. A higher dividend growth rate can also indicate that a company is rewarding its shareholders with increasing dividends, which can make it more appealing for income-seeking investors. Therefore, a higher dividend growth rate can result in a smaller ex-dividend date price drop, as fewer investors may sell the stock before the ex-dividend date to capture the dividend, and more investors may buy the stock on or after the ex-dividend date to benefit from the dividend.

3. **Market Conditions:** The market conditions are the overall state and trends of the stock market, such as bullish or bearish, volatile, or stable, etc. They reflect the general sentiment and expectations of investors and traders regarding the economy, industry, sector, and company. The market conditions can affect the demand and supply of stocks, as well as their prices and values. For example, in a bullish market, investors may be more optimistic and willing to buy stocks, which can drive up their prices and values. In a bearish market, investors may be more pessimistic and willing to sell stocks, which can drive down their prices and values. Therefore, the market conditions can influence the ex-dividend date price drop, as they can affect how investors perceive and react to dividends.

Options and Derivatives

Options and derivatives are financial instruments that derive their value from the underlying assets, such as stocks, bonds, commodities, currencies, etc. They can be used to enhance dividend trading by creating dividend income streams, hedging against risk, or speculating on price movements.

Options are contracts that give the buyer the right, but not the obligation, to buy or sell the underlying asset at a specified price (strike price) on or before a specified date (expiration date). The seller of the option receives a premium from the buyer for granting this right. There are two types of options: call and put. A call option gives the buyer the right to buy the underlying asset, while a put option gives the buyer the right to sell the underlying asset.

Basic Terminology

Some of the basic concepts and terminology of options are:

1. **Intrinsic Value:** The intrinsic value of an option is the difference between the current price of the underlying asset and the strike price of the option. It represents the profit that can be made by exercising the option. For example, if a call option has a strike price of $50 and the underlying asset is trading at $55, the intrinsic value of the option is $5.

2. **Extrinsic Value:** The extrinsic value of an option is the difference between the total price of the option (also known as the premium) and its intrinsic value. It represents the amount that the buyer pays for the time value and volatility of the option. For example, if a call option has a premium of $7 and an intrinsic value of $5, the extrinsic value of the option is $2.

3. **Delta:** The delta of an option is the rate of change in the option's price for a unit change in the price of the underlying asset. It measures how sensitive an option is to changes in the underlying asset's price. For example, if a call option has a delta of 0.6, it means that for every $1 increase in the underlying asset's price, the option's price will increase by $0.6.

4. **Gamma:** The gamma of an option is the rate of change in the option's delta with respect to a unit change in the price of the underlying asset. It measures how quickly an option's delta changes as the underlying asset's price changes. For example, if a call option has a gamma of 0.1, it means that for every $1 increase in the underlying asset's price, the option's delta will increase by 0.1.

5. **Theta:** The theta of an option is the rate of change in the option's price with respect to a unit change in time. It measures how much an option loses value as it approaches its expiration date. For example, if a call option has a theta of -0.05, it means that for every day that passes, the option's price will decrease by $0.05.

6. **Vega:** The Vega of an option is the rate of change in the option's price concerning a unit change in volatility. It measures how much an option gains or loses value as volatility changes. For example, if a call option has a Vega of 0.2, it means that for every 1% increase in volatility, the option's price will increase by $0.2.

Some examples of how to use options and derivatives to create dividend income streams, hedge against risk, or speculate on price movements are:

Creating Dividend Income Streams

One way to use options and derivatives to create dividend income streams is by selling covered call options on dividend-paying stocks. A covered call is a strategy where an investor sells a call option on a stock that he or she already owns. The investor collects the premium from selling the call option and also receives the dividend from owning the stock. However, if the stock price rises above the strike price of the call option by the expiration date, the investor will have to sell the stock at the strike price to the buyer of the call option and miss out on any further appreciation. Another way to use options and derivatives to create dividend income streams is by buying dividend futures or swaps. A dividend future is a contract that allows an investor to buy or sell a fixed amount of dividends from a stock or an index at a predetermined price and date in the future. A dividend swap is a contract that allows an investor to exchange one stream of dividends for another stream of dividends with different characteristics, such as frequency, amount, or currency. These contracts can help investors lock in future dividends or diversify their dividend sources.

Hedging Against Risk

One way to use options and derivatives to hedge against risk is by buying put options on dividend-paying stocks. A put option gives an investor the right to sell a stock at a specified price on or before a specified date. The investor pays a premium for this right. A put option can help an investor protect his or her downside risk from owning a stock that pays dividends, as the investor can exercise the put option and sell the stock at the strike price if the stock price falls below the strike price. The investor can also keep the dividend from owning the stock. However, if the stock price rises above the strike price, the investor will lose the premium paid for the put option and miss out on any further appreciation. Another way to use options and derivatives to hedge against risk is by using dividend collars or floors. A dividend collar is a strategy where an investor buys a put option and sells a call option on a dividend-paying stock with the same expiration date and different strike prices. The investor pays a lower premium for the put option by selling the call option but also limits his or her upside potential from owning the stock. A dividend collar can help an investor protect his or her dividend income and principal from large price movements in either direction. A dividend floor is a strategy where an investor buys a put option on a dividend-paying stock with a strike price equal to or lower than the expected dividend amount. The investor pays a premium for the put option but also guarantees his or her minimum dividend income regardless of the stock price. A dividend floor can help an investor hedge against dividend cuts or suspensions.

Speculating on Price Movements

One way to use options and derivatives to speculate on price movements is by buying call options on dividend-paying stocks. A call option gives an investor the right to buy a stock at a specified price on or before a specified date. The investor pays a premium for this right. A call option can help an investor leverage his or her bullish view on a stock that pays dividends, as the investor can exercise the call option and buy the stock at the strike price if the stock price rises above the strike price. The investor can also receive the dividend from owning the stock. However, if the stock price falls below the strike price, the investor will lose the premium paid for the call option and miss out on any dividends. Another way to use options and derivatives to speculate on price movements is by using dividend arbitrage or straddles. Dividend arbitrage is a strategy where an investor buys a stock before its ex-dividend date and sells a call option on it with a strike price equal to or lower than the expected dividend amount and an expiration date shortly after the ex-dividend date. The investor collects the dividend from owning the stock and also receives the premium from selling the call option. The investor hopes that the stock price will drop by less than or equal to the amount of the dividend on or after its ex-dividend date so that he or she can keep both the dividend and the premium without having to sell the stock to the buyer of the call option. Dividend arbitrage can help an investor exploit pricing inefficiencies between stocks and options around ex-dividend dates. A dividend straddle is a strategy where an investor buys a call option and a put option on a dividend-paying stock with the same expiration date and strike price. The investor pays a high premium for both options but also benefits from large price movements in either direction. The investor hopes that the stock price will move significantly before its ex-dividend date so that he or she can exercise one of the options and profit from it. Dividend straddle can help an investor take advantage of volatility and uncertainty around ex-dividend dates.

Advantages and Disadvantages

Options and derivatives have some advantages and disadvantages that investors should be aware of before using them. Some of these are:

1. **Leverage:** Options and derivatives can provide leverage for investors who want to amplify their returns from dividends. Leverage means that investors can control more assets with less capital, which can magnify their profits or losses. For example, buying a call option on a stock that pays dividends can allow an investor to benefit from both dividends and capital gains with less money than buying the stock outright.

2. **Flexibility:** Options and derivatives can offer flexibility for investors who want to customize their dividend trading strategies according to their objectives and expectations. Flexibility means that investors can choose different types, amounts, prices, dates, and combinations of options and derivatives to suit their needs and preferences. For example, using a dividend collar on a stock that pays dividends can allow an investor to protect his or her downside risk while limiting his or her upside potential.

3. **Complexity:** Options and derivatives can involve complexity for investors who need to understand their mechanics and implications. Complexity means that investors need to have sufficient knowledge, skills, experience, and tools to analyze and execute their options and derivatives transactions effectively and efficiently. For example, using a dividend swap on a stock that pays dividends can require an investor to understand how to value, monitor, and settle their swap contracts with their counterparties.

4. **Cost:** Options and derivatives can incur costs for investors who have to pay premiums, commissions, fees, taxes, etc. Cost means that investors need to consider how much they spend and how much they earn from their options and derivatives transactions. For example, buying a put option on a stock that pays dividends can require an investor to pay a premium for the option, which can reduce his or her net dividend income.

ETFs and Mutual Funds

ETFs and mutual funds are types of investment vehicles that allow investors to pool their money and invest in a diversified portfolio of securities, such as stocks, bonds, commodities, etc. They can be used to diversify a dividend portfolio by providing exposure to different sectors, regions, styles, and strategies that pay dividends.

ETFs and mutual funds have some differences and similarities that investors should be aware of before choosing them. Some of these are:

1. **Structure:** ETFs and mutual funds have different structures that affect how they are created, traded, and redeemed. ETFs are exchange-traded funds that trade like stocks on stock exchanges. They can be bought and sold throughout the day at market prices that fluctuate

based on supply and demand. ETFs are created and redeemed by authorized participants, who exchange a basket of underlying securities for ETF shares or vice versa. Mutual funds are open-end funds that trade at the end of the day at their net asset value (NAV), which is calculated based on the value of their underlying securities. Mutual funds are created and redeemed by fund managers, who issue or redeem fund shares directly to or from investors.

2. **Fees:** ETFs and mutual funds have different fees that affect their costs and returns. ETFs typically have lower fees than mutual funds, as they have lower operating expenses, management fees, and transaction costs. ETFs also have lower tax costs, as they generate fewer capital gains distributions than mutual funds. However, ETFs may incur brokerage commissions, bid-ask spreads, and premiums or discounts to NAV when buying or selling them. Mutual funds typically have higher fees than ETFs, as they have higher operating expenses, management fees, and transaction costs. Mutual funds also have higher tax costs, as they generate more capital gains distributions than ETFs. However, mutual funds may not incur brokerage commissions or bid-ask spreads when buying or selling them.

3. **Liquidity:** ETFs and mutual funds have different liquidity levels that affect their availability and price stability. ETFs generally have higher liquidity than mutual funds, as they can be traded throughout the day on stock exchanges. ETFs also have secondary market liquidity, which means that investors can buy or sell them from other investors without affecting the underlying securities. However, ETFs may face liquidity issues if there is low trading volume or high market volatility, which can widen the bid-ask spreads or create a premium or discount to NAV. Mutual funds generally have lower liquidity than ETFs, as they can only be traded at the end of the day at their NAV. Mutual funds also have primary market liquidity, which means that investors can only buy or sell them from the fund managers by affecting the underlying securities. However, mutual funds may face liquidity issues if there is high redemption pressure or low cash reserves, which can force fund managers to sell securities at unfavorable prices or impose redemption fees or gates.

4. **Performance:** ETFs and mutual funds have different performance outcomes that depend on their objectives and strategies. ETFs tend to track the performance of their underlying indexes or benchmarks more closely than mutual funds, as they have lower tracking errors and higher correlation. ETFs also tend to outperform mutual funds on a risk-adjusted basis, as they have lower fees and tax costs. However, ETFs may underperform mutual funds if there is high market volatility or inefficiency, which can create a premium or discount to NAV or divergence from the underlying index or benchmark. Mutual funds tend to deviate from the performance of their underlying indexes or benchmarks more than ETFs, as they have higher tracking errors and lower correlation. Mutual funds also tend to underperform ETFs on a risk-adjusted basis, as they have higher fees and tax costs. However, mutual funds may outperform ETFs if there is low market volatility or inefficiency, which can allow fund managers to use their active management skills or exploit market opportunities.

Examples

Some examples of some of the best ETFs and mutual funds for dividend investors are:

1. **Vanguard High Dividend Yield ETF (VYM)**: This is an ETF that tracks the performance of the FTSE High Dividend Yield Index, which consists of large-cap U.S. stocks that pay above-average dividends. The ETF has a yield of 3%, a growth rate of 7%, a quality score of 7 (out of 10), a sector exposure of 23% to financials, 13% to health care, 12% to consumer staples, and 10% to technology, and a dividend history of 14 years. The ETF has an expense ratio of 0.06%, which is very low compared to its category average of 0.4%.

2. **SPDR S&P Dividend ETF (SDY):** This is an ETF that tracks the performance of the S&P High Yield Dividend Aristocrats Index, which consists of mid-cap U.S. stocks that have increased their dividends for at least 25 consecutive years. The ETF has a yield of 2.7%, a growth rate of 6.5%, a quality score of 8 (out of 10), a sector exposure of 20% to industrials, 15% to financials, 14% to consumer staples, and 11% to materials, and a dividend history of 27 years. The ETF has an expense ratio of 0.35%, which is low compared to its category average of 0.4%.

3. **Fidelity Equity Dividend Income Fund (FEQTX):** This is a mutual fund that invests in large-cap U.S. stocks that pay above-average dividends and have the potential for capital appreciation. The fund has a yield of 2.8%, a growth rate of 6.8%, a quality score of 7 (out of 10), a sector exposure of 22% to financials, 16% to health care, 13% to consumer staples, and 12% to technology, and a dividend history of 23 years. The fund has an expense ratio of 0.61%, which is average compared to its category average of 0.61%.

4. **T. Rowe Price Dividend Growth Fund (PRDGX):** This is a mutual fund that invests in large-cap U.S. stocks that have a history of increasing their dividends and have the potential for long-term growth. The fund has a yield of 1.4%, a growth rate of 9.2%, a quality score of 9 (out of 10), a sector exposure of 25% to technology, 16% to health care, 15% to industrials, and 13% to consumer discretionary, and a dividend history of 24 years. The fund has an expense ratio of 0.64%, which is slightly higher than its category average of 0.61%.

Benefits and Drawbacks

Some benefits and drawbacks of ETFs and mutual funds are:

1. **Diversification:** ETFs and mutual funds can provide diversification for dividend investors by allowing them to invest in a basket of securities that pay dividends across different sectors, regions, styles, and strategies. Diversification can help reduce the risk and volatility of the portfolio, as well as increase the income and growth potential.

2. **Convenience**: ETFs and mutual funds can offer convenience for dividend investors by simplifying the investment process and reducing transaction costs. Convenience means that

investors can access a wide range of dividend-paying securities with one purchase or sale without having to research, analyze, monitor, or manage each individual security.

3. **Management Style:** ETFs and mutual funds can have different management styles that affect their performance and costs. Management style means that some ETFs and mutual funds are passively managed, which means that they follow a predefined index or benchmark with minimal intervention from the fund managers. Passive management can result in lower fees, lower tracking errors, and higher tax efficiency. Some ETFs and mutual funds are actively managed, which means that they deviate from a predefined index or benchmark with more intervention from the fund managers. Active management can result in higher fees, higher tracking errors, and lower tax efficiency.

4. **Tracking Error:** ETFs and mutual funds can have different tracking errors that affect their accuracy and consistency. Tracking error means the difference between the performance of an ETF or a mutual fund and its underlying index or benchmark. Tracking errors can be caused by various factors, such as fees, dividends, rebalancing, market conditions, etc. Tracking error can result in the underperformance or outperformance of an ETF or a mutual fund relative to its underlying index or benchmark.

5. **Expense Ratio:** ETFs and mutual funds can have different expense ratios that affect their costs and returns. The expense ratio is the annual fee that an ETF or a mutual fund charges its investors for managing the fund. The expense ratio can include various components, such as management fees, administrative fees, distribution fees, etc. The expense ratio can reduce the net return of an ETF or a mutual fund by lowering its NAV or premium.

ETFs and mutual funds are types of investment vehicles that can help dividend investors diversify their portfolios and achieve their financial goals. However, ETFs and mutual funds also have some differences and similarities that investors should consider before choosing them. Investors should also do their research and analysis on each ETF or mutual fund they plan to invest in concerning their objectives and expectations.

Chapter 10

Your Journey as a Dividend Stock Trader

By reading this book, you have gained a powerful tool to generate passive income, compound your returns, optimize your tax efficiency, and increase your capital appreciation. You have discovered the secrets and advantages of dividend stock trading that can help you achieve financial freedom and security. You have embarked on a journey that can transform your life and wealth for the better.

In this chapter, you will master how to reflect on your progress and growth as a dividend stock trader.

Celebrating Achievements and Reflecting on Progress

Whether you are just starting out or have been trading for a while, it's crucial to recognize the milestones and achievements you have reached. Perhaps you successfully built a diversified portfolio of dividend stocks, consistently received dividend payments, or achieved a specific financial target you set for yourself. These accomplishments are a testament to your dedication, perseverance, and growing expertise as a trader.

Take a look back at the significant milestones and achievements you have experienced on your journey as a dividend stock trader. Reflect on the moments that made you proud, such as the first dividend payment you received, reaching a certain percentage of return on investment, or successfully navigating through a challenging market period. By recognizing these milestones, you not only build confidence in your abilities but also gain motivation to continue progressing and improving your trading skills.

Even small achievements in dividend stock trading deserve celebration. Celebrating your successes, no matter how modest they may seem, is crucial for maintaining a positive mindset and staying motivated. Each step forward, no matter how small, brings you closer to your financial goals. Celebrating your progress not only boosts your confidence but also reinforces the positive habits and strategies you have developed along the way. So, take a moment to appreciate your accomplishments and acknowledge the hard work you have put into becoming a dividend stock trader.

As you celebrate your achievements, it's equally important to reflect on your personal growth and development as a dividend stock trader. Reflecting on the lessons you have learned and how they have shaped your trading approach will help you gain valuable insights and continue evolving as an investor.

Consider the lessons you have learned throughout your journey. What were the pivotal moments that taught you valuable insights about dividend stock trading? Reflect on the mistakes you made, the risks you took, and the successful trades you executed. Each experience provides an opportunity for growth and learning. By reflecting on these lessons, you can identify patterns, refine your strategies, and adjust your approach accordingly.

Self-awareness is a key component of personal growth and development as a dividend stock trader. By understanding your strengths, weaknesses, and areas for improvement, you can make conscious efforts to enhance your trading skills. Embrace a mindset of continuous improvement, seeking out new knowledge, and staying open to different perspectives. Cultivating a growth mindset will enable you to adapt to changing market conditions and seize new opportunities.

As you reflect on your progress and personal growth, it's essential to revisit and evaluate your financial goals. The knowledge and experience you have gained as a dividend stock trader may have influenced your perspective on what is achievable and realistic.

Take the time to assess the progress you have made toward your initial financial goals. Have you reached the milestones you set for yourself?

Are you on track to achieve your long-term objectives?

By evaluating your progress, you can gain a clearer understanding of where you stand and identify any areas that may need adjustment.

As you reflect on your journey, you may discover that your goals need to be adjusted or refined. The knowledge and experience you have gained as a dividend stock trader might have given you new insights into what is realistic and attainable. Be open to modifying your financial goals based on this newfound knowledge. Adjusting your goals can help ensure that they align with your current understanding of the market and your capabilities as a trader.

The Power of Persistence in Growing Income and Wealth

When discussing the long-term nature of dividend stock investing, it is important to emphasize two key aspects: the compounding effect of reinvesting dividends and the importance of patience and long-term thinking. By reinvesting dividends back into additional shares of dividend-paying stocks, investors can experience the power of compounding over time. This compounding effect allows for exponential growth as both the stock price and the dividend payouts increase. However, it is essential to remind readers that this growth takes time and requires a patient mindset. Short-term market fluctuations are inevitable, but by maintaining a long-term perspective, investors can reap the rewards of consistent dividend payouts and capital appreciation.

Maximizing income and wealth through dividend stocks involves implementing effective strategies. One such strategy is exploring different dividend reinvestment strategies and understanding their benefits. Dividend reinvestment plans (DRIPs) allow investors to automatically reinvest dividends into additional shares of the same company. This approach harnesses the power of compounding and can accelerate wealth accumulation. Additionally, diversifying a dividend stock portfolio is crucial for maximizing income and managing risk. By spreading investments across multiple sectors and industries, investors can mitigate the impact of market volatility. Implementing risk management techniques and considering factors such as dividend yield, dividend growth, and financial stability when selecting dividend stocks can further enhance income streams and long-term growth.

Conclusion

In conclusion, this book has provided a comprehensive guide to dividend stock trading for beginners looking to grow their income and generate tremendous profit. By explaining the fundamentals of dividend investing, identifying high-quality dividend stocks, the power of dividend reinvestment, crafting trading strategies, mitigating risks, optimizing taxes, and overcoming psychological pitfalls, this book has equipped readers with the knowledge and skills to thrive as dividend stock traders.

The key takeaways include understanding how dividends can produce income and growth, leveraging compounding through dividend reinvestment plans, conducting a thorough analysis of dividend safety and quality, developing customized trading strategies aligned with goals and risk tolerance, and cultivating the proper psychology and expectations. While dividend trading does carry some risks, they can be managed through prudence, discipline, and continuing education.

Overall, by internalizing the timeless principles and proven best practices outlined in this book and applying them diligently, dividend stock trading can offer beginners a powerful vehicle for generating tremendous profit through a growing stream of passive income. The journey requires commitment, patience, adaptability, and perspective, but the rewards can last a lifetime. There has never been a better time to take control of your financial future through dividend stock investing.

References

White, H. Economic prediction using neural networks: The case of IBM daily stock returns. In: IEEE International Conference on Neural Networks. San Diego, 1988, pp. 451-459.

Lowe, A.R.Webb. Time series prediction by adaptive networks: a dynamical systems perspective. In Artificial Neural Networks: Forecasting Time Series (eds. V. Rao Vemuri and Robert D. Rogers). IEEE Computer Society Press, 1994, pp. 12-19. D.

F. Fama. Efficient capital markets, Journal of Finance, 46(5),1991, 1575-1617.

D.J. Baestaens, W.M. van den Bergh, H. Vaudrey. Market inefficiencies, technical trading, and neural networks. In: Dunis, C. (ed.): Forecasting Financial Markets, Financial Economics and Quantitative Analysis, Chichester, John Wiley & Sons, 1996, pp. 245-260.

A.Refenes. Neural Networks in the Capital Markets, Wiley, Chichester, 1995.

W. Leigh, R. Purvis, J.M. Ragusa. Forecasting the NYSE composite index with technical analysis, pattern recognizer, neural network, and genetic algorithm: a case study in romantic decision support. Decision Support Systems, 32, 2002, 361-377.

H. Hong. J. Stein. A unified theory of underreaction, momentum trading, and overreaction in asset markets, The Journal of Finance LIV (6), 1999, 2143-2184.

H. Hong, T. Lim, J. Stein. Bad news travels slowly: size, analyst coverage, and the profitability of momentum strategies. The Journal of Finance LV (1), 2000, 265-295.

S.B. Achelis. Technical Analysis from A to Z, 2nd Editon, McGraw-Hill Professional,

2000.

R. Martinelli, B. Hyman. Cup-with-handle and the computerized approach. Technical Analysis of Stocks and Commodities, 16(10), 1999, 63-66.

Sharpe W. F. Asset allocation: Management Style and Performance Measurement," Journal of Portfolio Management, Winter 1992, pp. 7-19